Restoration Earth

An Interdisciplinary Journal for the Study of Nature & Civilization

2011 Volume 1, Issue 1

Editors

Katherine E. Batten (MacDowell), D.Th.

Dean, Ocean Seminary College

Mark A. Schroll, PhD

Research Adjunct Faculty,
Institute of Transpersonal Psychology

Tanya Collings

Assistant Editor

Contact

oceanseminary@verizon.net
rockphd4@yahoo.com
(for inquiries and article submissions)

Published by Ocean Seminary College & the International Association for Transpersonal Ecosophy
http://www.facebook.com/RestorationEarth
http://www.oceanseminarycollege.org
http://www.IATranspersonalEcosophy.org

Restoration Earth is published twice per year: May 15th and November 15th on thematic/subject issues. Please see the above noted websites for current call for papers. All disciplines are encouraged to submit. Authors engaged in academic research should follow APA style, if possible. File formats accepted: doc, docx, jpg, png, pdf, bmp. Graphics being submitted should be at least 300px. If you are interested in editing a special issue or would like more information on the journal, please contact Dr. Batten MacDowell or Dr. Schroll for information.

On our cover: UFFINGTON HORSE copyright © 2010 by Anne Westlund. Anne created the image on the coast off the Pacific Ocean in Washington State. Her process notes were as follows:

August 18, 2010, low tide, at the beach about 2:30 pm. The beach was busy—August. No one paid me any mind or commented on my beach drawing. I went down there with my mom so she could take pictures of me doing the drawing. That didn't work out: She struck up a conversation with a perfect stranger. About 66-degrees at the beach; I have a bad cold, but the ocean breeze feels good. I made a much smaller version of the horse geoglyph [Anne was exploring what it may have felt like to create the actual geoglyph found in Great Britain] from a picture I printed off the internet. Cool! I love making things, even if temporary. Low tide, with the tide coming in. I like knowing that it's already gone; disappeared into the waves…

Restoration Earth

An Interdisciplinary Journal for the Study of Nature & Civilization
2011 Volume 1, Issue 1

Table of Contents

Contributing Photographers: Anne Westlund, Chris Westlund, Katherine Batten (MacDowell)

Remembering Indigenous Mind

Mark A. Schroll

Schroll, M.A. (2011). Remembering Indigenous Mind. *Restoration Earth: An Interdisciplinary Journal for the Study of Nature & Civilization*, 1(1), 1–3. Copyright © The Authors. All rights reserved. For reprint information contact: oceanseminary@verizon.net.

Part 1. The 21ˢᵗ Century Urban Dweller

Late one hot summer night,
I listened to the constant wail of sirens,
The roar of traffic outside my window,
And the familiar shouting of my neighbors arguing.
Perhaps that is the way they relate before their banter turns into sex,
Or could this be a form of foreplay to establish their roles of dominance and submission,
Or perhaps they are just watching TV.
Fact and fantasy are often difficult to separate.
Is it life that imitates art, or is it art that imitates life?
Or does the fabric of our existential lives weave
The thread of artistic expression via a
Reflexive co-creation?
Am I generating this text and thereby creating new meaning,
Or are these symbolic expressions of sound and silence no more
Than chaotic reconstructions without any purpose other than
That which we ascribe to it?
Contemplating this enigmatic crossroads in search of reality
There was at least one thing of which I was certain,
I could no longer stand the creeping sensation of sweat
That continued to trickle down my back,
An experience of torment that was intensified by
The sticky humid breezes carrying the smell of rotting garbage
Through the open widows of my apartment,
Whose aroma clung to my sweat-soaked skin like some primordial perfume.
Seeking relief, I chose to take a drive in the country.

Part 2. Inner City Angst and a Journey into the Unknown

Upon leaving the city limits,
Beyond the trance of this human constructed mythos
That we have breathed into existence with our narrative metaphors,
Beyond the glare of buzzing neon lights
That try to keep us a willing slave to their flashing symbols of consumerism,
Like zombie grubs feeding on the material structures of technology
In cinematic homage to the Night of the Living Dead and Neo-Darwinian dreams
While those who wish they had the courage to be heroes are
Secretly hoping to awaken from this nightmare and breakthrough
The chrysalis as butterflies—free to explore the farther reaches of cognition,
While the antihero watches this scene of self-projected iconic archetypal wannabe heroes

Hoping that at least for a timeless moment of this every present now
There will at least not be some crisis crying out for help.
And then all this deafening noise and senseless chatter begins to cease as
The arrogance of my self-centered humanism slowly begins to fade from my awareness.
Gradually the messages to consume, consume, consume
Ease their pounding tension within my body/mind.
Pulling my car to the side of the road, I stop.
Stepping out of my car, stepping out the limits of self,
I turn my gaze to the night sky,
Observing its mysterious grandeur.

Part 3: Confronting Nature's Fearful Unknowns

Feeling refreshed,
Like having thrown off a great weight that had been holding me down
I get back into my car, back into the vehicle of my body and personality construct.
This experience marks my journey's beginning.
Soon the landscape changes,
As I continue to motor on beneath the sheer rock faces of a canyon wall,
Brightly illuminated by a full moon's glow.
The boulders of the canyon seem to gaze upon me
Like stone gargoyles perched on reptilian legs,
Ready to strike at the unwary passersby below—nature grinning with fangs red
As I cringe with fear.

Part 4: Cosmic Unity and Transpersonal Awakening

As the valley deepens
The walls of the canyon loom every larger
While the rhythm of my tires beat out sounds as they pound the pavement,
Liken to a ceremonial drumbeat
Whose resounding echo fills the maze of canyon walls in endless reverberation.
Onward, onward, relentlessly proceeding onward
Twisting and turning on endless curves,
As my car's headlights blaze like beacons illuminating the secrets lying before me,
As the rubber roadway snakes out far into the night.

Gradually the magic of this solitude
Mixed with the continual pounding rhythm of my tires,
Send my thoughts racing into the inner recesses of my unconscious,
Filling my body/mind with scenes of passionate demonstrations of Eros,
Skyclad dancers of many colors around a large bonfire,
Herds of wild animals of every description,
Fertile plains, mountains, glaciers, meadows,
Streams, rivers, seas, and oceans teeming with life,
Gaseous clouds of cosmic debris,

Exploding nebula,
Then the boundary between these scenes and my consciousness melds together
Becoming a unified field of experience.
Timespace and selfhood dissolves.

Part 5: The Return: Fading Vision or Motivation for Transformation?

Flying sparks and the sound of metal
Scraping against rock brings me rushing back into normal consciousness,
As I and thou are torn asunder once again
And that which had for so brief a moment been joined in harmonious unity
Is now one more division, separation, alienation, aloneness,
While my grip tightens on the wheel (of life),
I manage at the last second to wrestle my car back onto the roadway
As the cinema of this postmodern drama begins to play anew
While the glow of my vision fades like a dream.

How can I keep this dream alive within me?
How can I hold its memory in my awareness?
For in place of its imagery are the lights of the city,
Shining in the distance.
Calling me back with its siren song,
Calling me back to consume, consume, consume,
Calling me back to the place that humankind calls civilization.

MARK A. SCHROLL, Ph.D., Research Adjunct Faculty, Institute of Transpersonal Psychology, Palo Alto, California, and serves on the Advisory Board of *Alternative Therapies in Health and Medicine*. He served as Guest Managing Editor of the special *Anthropology of Consciousness*, *22*(1), 2011 issue "From Primordial Anthropology to a Transpersonal Ecosophy", and *Anthropology of Consciousness*, *16*(1), 2005 issue "Primordial Visions in an Age of Technology". He co-chaired the 2009 "Bridging Nature and Human Nature" annual Society for the Anthropology of Consciousness conference co-sponsored by the Association for Transpersonal Psychology. He serves on the Editorial Board of *Paranthropology: Journal of Anthropological Approaches to the Paranormal*. He serves on the Windbridge Institute Scientific Advisory Board. He was the Founding Editor of *Rhine Online: Psi-News Magazine*. He Edited *Rhine Online*, *3*(1), 2011, the special 2nd-anniversary issue "Sacred Sites, Consciousness, and the Eco-Crisis". He serves on the Editorial Board of *Goddess Thealogy: An International Journal for the Study of Feminism and Religion* and the Board of the Institute for Thealogy and Deasophy. He has been invited to serve as the Co-Editor of the 1st issue of *Goddess Thealogy* with Patricia 'Iolana (In Press). Schroll is a transpersonal cultural theorist and conference organizer with multi-disciplinary interests ranging from philosophy of science to transpersonal ecosophy. Contact: rockphd4@yahoo.com

"Seal Pup" copyright © 2011 by Anne Westlund. Photo taken in Washington State, USA.

Editors' Introduction:

Understanding the Transpersonal

Ecosophical Perspective

Katherine E. Batten (MacDowell) and Mark A. Schroll

Batten (MacDowell), K. E., & Schroll, M.A. (2011). Editors' introduction: Understanding the transpersonal ecosophical perspective. *Restoration Earth: An Interdisciplinary Journal for the Study of Nature & Civilization, 1*(1), 5–18. Copyright © The Authors. All rights reserved. For reprint information contact: oceanseminary@verizon.net.

> "... *human population explosion, destructive technologies, global*
> *warming; a crash in food supply; [etc] . . . . It all sounds so familiar*
> *because it is the environmental holocaust that we fear may befall our*
> *children in the twenty-first century",* yet according to Jared Diamond
> these are the contributing factors that may have caused the collapse in the
> civilization of Cro-Magnon more than 11,000 years ago (Diamond, 1993, p. 29).

Introduction

Choose any date within the last 100 years that you think the eco-crisis and all of its related social ills started (moving backwards from today this would take you back as far as 1911) and you will find that we need to go even further back to find the source of today's problems. According to Diamond (1993) we would need to go back more than 11,000 years to find the source of the eco-crisis and our modern social ills. It is thus an understatement of millennial proportions to say humankind has been ignoring the warning signs of how to live in relationship to each other and the nonhuman world. We have ignored them for thousands of years.

Reflecting on whether or not it would require an equal amount of time to reverse our present situation calls to mind the haunting lyrics of the song "In the Year 2525", by Lincoln, Nebraska's musical duo Denny Zager and Rick Evans. On July 20, 1969, it reached number one on the Billboard charts; that same day, as it played on radios across the USA, Neil Armstrong and Buzz Aldrin took the first walk on the moon. As if to put this technological achievement and the direction our human societies were (and continue) moving rapidly towards into greater perspective, the lyrics read:

> In the year 2525
> If man is still alive
> If woman can survive
> They may find . . .
> ***
> In the year 9595
> I'm kinda wondering if man is gonna be alive
> He's taken everything this old earth can give
> And he ain't put back nothing
> Now it's been 10,000 years
> Man has cried a billion tears
> For what he never knew
> Now man's reign is through
> But through eternal night
> The twinkling of starlight
> So very far away
> Maybe it's only yesterday

"Maybe it's only yesterday" is Zager and Evans hopeful message, bringing us to the point of this Introduction that the time we need to be concerned about doing something to address the eco-crisis and its related social ills is now! Indeed this is the only time and place that we can begin, informed by the successes and mistakes of the past, combined with as much hope for the future as we can call together in our visions, and hold these visions in our hearts as the guiding principles of *Logos* and *Eros* (explored in greater depth shortly). The uneasy détente that has existed between these two perspectives throughout human history (Tarnas, 1991; Schroll & Greenwood, 2011) is reaching a point where more and more people are considering the need to renegotiate this armistice, as David Ray Griffin (1988) points out:

> The conviction is growing that science is not a value-free enterprise or, to put it more precisely, that values other than the purely intellectual value of truth for its own sake, and that factors other than rational and empirical ones, essentially shape the worldview of the scientific community. Of course, it has long been recognized that the scientific community is composed of human beings, so that the same types of distortion, projection, power plays, and other nonrational factors operate in it as in other communities. But it was assumed, as classically formulated by Thomas Merton, that science as a social system, in which these nonrational factors operate, can be separated from science as a cognitive system, which is governed by logic and empirical facts. Science as a cognitive system was thought to be essentially value-free, except for those values that are internal to science itself, i.e., its distinctive way of pursuing truth. But now it is widely held that this separation is not possible and that social factors affect science essentially, not just superficially. Rather than standing as an impartial tribunal of truth, transcendent over the battlefield of competing social forces, science is seen as one more interested participant, using its status to legitimate certain social, political, and economic forces and to illegitimate others. More than that, the scientific community's interest in its own social power relative to other professions and institutions is now seen to condition the picture of the world it sanctions as "scientific". (p. 8–9)

Assuming Griffin's (1988) assessment is correct it is now more important than ever for us to be aware how cultural (scientific and religious) assumptions shape our expectations. As recently as 500 years ago ancient mariners who believed the Earth was flat feared the possibility of sailing to the edge of the Earth and falling off. Now we laugh at this flat Earth theory, and yet our current cosmological views are still very new. It was only 92 years ago that Einstein's theories of spacetime received astronomical confirmation, proving his General Theory of Relativity. Still Einstein failed to believe his own mathematical calculations that suggested the universe was expanding, because the prevailing assumption at this time believed the universe to be a stable or steady-state entity. This prevailing assumption was shown to be incorrect by 1923 based on the astronomical data of Edwin Hubble, proving the universe was indeed expanding (Gribbin, 1986; Jeans, 1943/1981). Further examples could be given to illustrate how our assumptions of reality have influenced our scientific, cultural, and religious views (Bohm & Peat, 1987; Davies, 1983; Toulmin, 1982). But hopefully these few examples we have mentioned make the point that many widely held assumptions and metaphors continue to shape our worldview that we tend to treat as facts.

Humankind's tendency to "take the metaphors of our own culture as truths" (Lakoff & Johnson, 1980, p. 186), prompted Thomas Berry[1] to suggest we need to "re-invent the human at the species level" (Metzner: 1999, p. 171); we need to reexamine our scientific, religious and cultural assumptions. In other words, Berry (1988; see also Metzner, 1999) is calling us all to collectively reexamine the myths, metaphors and stories that we have woven together to create the tapestry of Euro–American science and our own *personal mythological* interpretations.[2]

---

[1] In Berry's own words he said: "We must invent, or reinvent, a sustainable human culture by a descent into our pre-rational, our instinctive, resources. Our cultural resources have lost their integrity. They cannot be trusted. What is needed is not transcendence but "inscendence" not the brain but the gene" (Berry, 1988, p. 207–208).

[2] David Feinstein and Stanley Krippner (1988) point out: "Your *personal mythology* may be thought of as the system of complementary and contradictory personal myths that organizes your sense of reality and guides your actions. The theme at the core of a personal myth is a composite, usually built from many sources" (p. 24). Elaborating on this definition Feinstein and Krippner tell us:

> A personal myth is a constellation of beliefs, feelings, and images that is organized around a core theme and addresses one of the domains within which mythology traditionally functions. According to Joseph Campbell, these include: (1) the urge to

Likewise James Hillman and Michael Ventura (1992) suggest in their book *We've Had A Hundred Years of Psychotherapy and the World's Getting Worse* that this need to reinvent the human at the species level is the means humankind may use to survive the shipwreck of Euro–American science, religion, and culture. Shipwreck is a metaphor that Hillman and Ventura use to help us come to grips with the death of Western civilization. "To put it a little less darkly", says Ventura, Western civilization's death is a reference to the fact that "it's transforming such that you won't be able to call it Western civilization anymore" (p. 225). Elaborating on this metaphor, Ventura argues:

> We in the West don't have a vision of this dying civilization joining the collective memory and heritage of the race, where it would feed the human heritage long after its time, as other civilizations have done. Instead we see the death of Western civilization as an absolute ending in which we have to justify all our history—so we fake and lie a lot and wave flags—and which will probably (so we tend to think) bring the end of the entire world. (p. 226)

We see this happening now with the rise of the Tea Party movement, calling for us to take back America. These well-meaning people are expressing the same fears as ancient mariners who begged Columbus to turn back lest they reach the end of the Earth and fall off. The end of the world myth (otherwise known as the myth of Armageddon) also highlights these issues. The myth of Armageddon tells us our time on Earth is limited; it tells us there is a linear progression of processes and events leading to a final endpoint beyond the ability of humans to have any influence to change it. This is why the Tea Party movement so desperately wants to take America back to something that they know how to control. It is the psychological need for social conformity—the herd bunches up—as this need for conformity increases due to fears of collapse, dismemberment, and death. Furthermore this myth serves to foster a fatalistic attitude whereby we tell ourselves that once we pass a certain point we will be powerless to change course. Leading us to believe that there is nothing we can do to influence our lives and the events of our future. Similar ideas are reflected in concepts held by mainstream environmentalists such as the concern about the Earth's "carrying capacity", which can be understood as a variation of René Thom's (1975) catastrophe theory.[3]

All this leads to our inaugural issue of *Restoration Earth: Interdisciplinary Journal for the Study of Nature and Civilization* in which we contemplate the question: what lies beyond Western civilization? More specifically (or more practical and action-oriented) we ask: How can we envision a new story of science, religion, the nature of humanity, and of our relationship to the rest of life on earth that will help us create a coherent, co-evolutionary, sustainable culture?

Logos and Eros Revisited as a Guide to *Restoration Earth*

In our endeavor to welcome all of us into becoming involved as co-researchers toward a reinvention of cultural products (science, religion, humanities, the arts, etc.), we will seek (as much as it is possible within the conventions of language) to avoid arguing truth claims. Instead the theories and practices discussed in *Restoration Earth* shall be introduced by proposing various theses, perspectives, or proposals. In choosing this approach, we are attempting to make visible the important differences between the ways of knowing associated with *Logos* and *Eros*, while also striving to locate a balance between these perspectives.

---

comprehend the natural world in a meaningful way; (2) the search for a marked pathway through the succeeding epochs of human life; (3) the need to establish secure and fulfilling relationships within a community; and (4) the longing to know one's part in the vast wonder and mystery of the cosmos. Personal myths explain the world, guide personal development, provide social direction, and address spiritual longings in a manner that is analogous to the way cultural myths carry out those functions for entire societies. Personal myths do for an individual what cultural myths do for a community. (p. 24)

[3] According to Ilay Prigogine and Isabelle Stengers (1984), Thom's concept of catastrophe theory is representative of a worldview that envisions every event as "determined by initial conditions that were, at least in principle, determinable with precision. It was a world in which chance played no part, in which all the pieces came together like cogs in a cosmic machine" (Prigogine & Stengers, p. xiii). At the International Wittgenstein Sym-

What Is Meant by Logos?

We raise the issue of *Logos* into awareness because arguing a point of view creates a philosophical and social–psychological environment that becomes polemical, and thereby potentially hostile to other ways of knowing. Polemical speech attempts to convince its audiences that what is being presented is the *correct* or *winning* point of view. Implicit within this epistemological framework is that all other points of view *must* be either wrong or imperfect and thereby suffer the humiliation of being considered the loser in an argument. Granted the *Logos*-orientated perspective does include, within its means of thesis justification (or its points of view), antithesis (or counterpoints of view) and synthesis (bringing these points of view together); all the time, however, there is a very conscious presence of winning and losing associated with this mode of knowing. This is especially evident in the political system of the world's so-called democracies, whose tangled web of reasoning has evolved into both a conscious atmosphere of compromise coupled with purposefully structured threats to basic needs in the formation of many policy decisions and implementations. Political negotiators are acutely conscious of this art of compromise and psychological posturing, which might be best expressed as: how much ground would one give up and who will best persuade the public that a political position is more likely to secure their basic needs that are framed as threatened by the competing party? In an effort to define the *Logos*-oriented perspective, June Singer (1990) tells us:

> The person in whom Logos is a guiding principle tends to view the world through logical, rational processes. Such an individual tends to be highly verbal, often intellectual, and needs to have a reason or an explanation before accepting something as valid or true. If this person is convinced of the rightness of a position, no effort will be spared in putting it forth and standing up for it. Because this person's own self-esteem depends largely on being correct or accurate, on seeking the truth in whatever form it may be found, and on expressing that truth in the most cogent forms possible, he or she does not feel a great need for the approval of others. Consequently, Logos people often find themselves to be in isolated postures, and they may be loners or have only a very few intimate and supportive friends. (p.14)

The psychological construct of *Logos*-oriented inquiry is full of implicit assumptions about ownership, boundary lines, and gaining and losing ground. *Logos*-oriented inquiry can therefore be summed up as an investigative procedure that follows the rules of a finite game, whose purpose, according to James P. Carse (1986) author of *Finite and Infinite Games*, is a contest played for victory or defeat. This is a method of inquiry that is exclusive and contrary to the principles of synthesis and cooperation; entrenching individuals into camps of right and wrong and thus creating divisions between individuals, groups of individuals, and cultures. *Logos* as the lone, structuring epistemology perpetuates a persisting and dynamic tension of worldviews in collision—a process this journal seeks to move away from. To move toward a possible alternative Joseph Meeker (1997) points out in his book *The Comedy of Survival*:

> In an infinite game, the only purpose of the game is to prevent it from coming to an end, and to keep everyone in play. . . . It can be found in the play of children and of animals, in enduring love, in evolution and natural selection, in symbiosis and cooperation of all kinds, and in those forms of behavior that are so satisfying that we want them to go on and on. (p. 1–18)

This is not to say that every idea is true or that every perspective provides a right answer—otherwise known as cultural relativism—or that we have been able to completely refrain from referring to the discussion of the proposals made in *Restoration Earth* as particular points of view. What is being suggested is that the way in which we have sought to approach the theories and practices discussed in *Restoration Earth* begins from the perspective of a dialogue, where people are actively involved in searching for the truth collectively, drawing their knowledge from a variety of sources, cultures, and points of view. This method of communi-

---

posium, Kirchberg am Wechsel, D. B. Linskey (from Bonn, Germany) and I (Schroll) had the opportunity to speak briefly with Thom. Defending his views and expressing his doubts towards the credibility of a nonlocal universe, which Prigogine's dissapative structures represented, which he felt was an inaccurate description of far-from-equilibrium conditions and that Rupert Sheldrake's views of morphogenesis were simply crazy (personal communication, August 11, 1986).

cation (guided by the ways of knowing associated with *Eros*) is inclusive, and thereby nurtures and facilitates integration, cooperation, and the creative unfolding of new ideas associated with worldviews in metamorphosis. "Eros-oriented people", as Singer (1990) points out:

> . . . are quite at home with human relationships, and, in fact, desperately need them. Such people will go to almost any length to avoid causing pain to another person—not so much out of generosity as out of fear of being abandoned. They are compassionate and thoughtful, and find it tempting to put aside their personal needs or beliefs in favor of being loved by another. For the Eros-oriented person, the world of Logos seems nearly inaccessible. (p. 14)

In seeking to move away from this exclusive perspective of *Logos*-oriented knowing, *Restoration Earth* seeks to question the ways of knowing that Euro–American science has constructed in terms of our *normal range of consciousness*; the usual states and stations of awareness that we have come to associate with our physical world; it is an invitation for us to begin peeling back the layers of our conceptual constructs, to look deep within ourselves, to waken within us a sense of alarm that will motivate us to begin this process of restructuring our vision of reality and our existing methods of inquiry. This invitation to begin a multicultural dialogue to reinvent culture and its products (such as science, religion, art, humanities) is a means to try and move away from dominant discourses, by learning how to value all sides of the human story. It is an attempt to remind us that our *Logos*-oriented way of knowing is simply one of a plurality of possible ways of knowing or states of consciousness that are useful in our pursuit of understanding the experiences, parameters, responsibilities, and limitations of being alive on Earth—of our embedded and interconnected existence. It is an attempt to tell the *whole* story of humankind's evolving narrative construction concerning the passage of time upon this earth, rather than a story distorted by political, social, economic, and psychological motives. And telling this complete story of our universe also includes telling the story of an inclusive world whose voice is not defined by singular human speech and experience of a singular monolithic culture, but rather defined by a range of voices (Schroll & Walker, 2011). Voices of creatures whose lives hang in the balance of existence as Western and Westernized cultures determine their value and thus their rights to exist (a process equally visible in the increasing dissolution of smaller, indigenous cultures as larger cultures subsume them). And this complete story is also one that gives voice to human and nonhuman individuals and groups who have been entirely lost under the foot of human "progress", from the reshaping of natural landscapes to acquire more material wealth and goods at the expense of a community of individuals currently thriving in those environments to more extreme expressions such as genocide and extinction (Schroll & Walker, 2011).

Seeking Unity: Restoring Eros to Logos

Philosopher Renee Weber (1986) has asked:

"[Is] the search for unity in science itself a spiritual path? My hypothesis is that it is." (p.13)

Considered the oldest form of loosely organized and systematized religious behavior (Parrinder, 1983), shamanism[4] not only remains the central religious structure to numerous cultures worldwide, but has become an increasingly popular mode of transpersonal experience within Western cultures (see Harvey, 2003). Characterized broadly as including, to varying degrees: (a) the presence of a personal and beneficial relationship between shaman and nonphysical being (whether nonhuman animal, deceased ancestor, or spirit); (b) a cosmological, multiverse structure through which the shaman moves to obtain knowledge or healing by entering into an altered state of consciousness; and (c) a belief in an interconnectivity and interdependence between self, community, and other living species coupled with perspectives that the very landscape is inhabited by a larger consciousness (such as a deity or ancestor spirit or nature spirit) that requires respect

---

4 It is important to note that while shamanism is utilized in this article to describe cross-cultural phenomena that may be characterized by shared features; the authors of this article recognize that this assertion should be viewed with critical skepticism. Numerous writers have criticized early anthropological work such as Eliade's as misrepresenting shamanistic-based practices creating an *illusion* of sameness or outright culturally constructing shamanism itself. Further critics are also quick to point out that the Western neo-shamanism movement must be carefully examined for the

(Eliade, 1954/1964; Vitebsky, 2001). These characteristics, which emphasize interdependency between other living beings and an orientation belief that humans dwell *within* Nature, coupled with the seemingly innate capacity/potentiality within human beings to *experience* this interdependency through natural and/or ritualistic methods to transform one's immediate state of consciousness, has contributed to the reemergence of shamanism in Western societies as a viable counterpoint to the prevailing *Logos*-based narratives, which may be best described by Yunt (2001):

> ...that for many people [referring specifically to Westerners and Western-influenced cultures] today, the world is seen as an inert, passive substance that conforms to our reason and expectations but that has no concomitant impact on our mind; in this unidirectional causality, we act on nature, but nature does not act on us. . . . [O]ur modern understanding of the world makes it difficult for many to grasp the relationship between what happens in our psyche and what occurs "out there" in the material world of nature. In fact, our understanding of the world is still largely grounded in Kantian (limits of subjectivity), Cartesian (mind–nature dualism), and Newtonian (mechanistic) assumptions about the psyche and its relationship to events and objects in the world. The relationship between what the mind conceives and the consequences these conceptions have on shaping the world often go unseen, or, in our age of manufacturing perceptions with the aid of psychological insights, these psyche–nature relationships are misconstrued for reasons of convenience or profit. (p. 99–100)

Shamanism has come to be seen as a counterpoint to this pervasive disconnection of Western civilization to the planet—an alternative way of meaning making that offers the possibility of hope. Schroll (2011) writes: "the shaman's purpose for exploring these worlds, or expanded states of consciousness, is to bring healing insights and energies of those realms back into this world" (p. 33). The transformation of consciousness that allows the shaman to encounter a multiverse and experience interdependency naturally locates shamanism as an experience born of *Eros* (discussed in more depth shortly). And to that point, shamanism is widely ignored by science, diminished as a "primitive" or "proto-" or less evolved illegitimate religious orientation, or outright pathologized as evidence of mental illness (Krippner, 2002; see also Eliade, for a discussion on the theory of psychiatric pathology and the shamanic experience; see Wright, 2009, as an example of an evolutionary framing of religion).

There is a deeper reason that Euro–American science continues to ignore the importance and viability of shamanism in our lives as one potential way to reorient ourselves to the world around us and that is specifically linked to the deliberate, although now unconscious, absenting of an *Eros* way of knowing. The *Logos* worldview of sciences is tied to Medieval Augustinian Christian theological legacy that (in brief): (a) demonized the body as innately sinful and thus sex was strictly for procreation, while the capacity to deny one's sexual urges was viewed as embodying greater spiritual status, (b) amplified a Greek philosophical belief that physical existence was punishment and the only hope of joy and peace would come only *after* one was liberated from the Earth itself; (c) allocated blame of the suffering of the human condition to women and thus systematically removed them from equal social standing (indeed medical sciences have only recently begun to specifically look at women's health as distinct having long-since conducted research only on men assuming women's biological functions were simply an extension of men's—Eve as a rib of Adam); and (d) established an order of life whereby human beings were placed above all other species and the natural world was *given* to and *created for men*. This legacy has made us loathe what in fact makes us uniquely human: our sexuality, which is fundamentally connected with our symbolic representation of self and other.

Sex for humans is not merely for procreation, it is a marvelous gift of recreation: "Re-creation". It is a form of play that allows us to show each other how much we care about the significant others whose lives we touch. What a sad commentary on the history of humankind and our relationship to all natural systems that requires us to hide what is truly a thing of beauty, transforming it into ugliness and shame. Instead of celebrating this wondrous gift of *Eros*, we tend to lock it away within ourselves through our guilt, believing that we have fallen victim to a darkness that has descended onto our soul. And even here we encounter a

---

possibility of cultural exportation and Western colonization practices (see Harvey, General Introduction, 2003). The intention of the authors in this article is to simply provide a tangible example of the beneficial possibility of such a worldview structure towards reshaping Western orientations towards the natural world, each other, and other species.

further problem in the very concept of soul, which carries with it so much emotional baggage that we fail to remember it refers to Psyche, the breath of life and the beautiful woman with whom Cupid fell in love. To avoid confusion, and to eliminate the necessity for our review of this story from Greek mythology, a better term for soul is *Eros*.

Eros is the power of visionary experience, of intuition, of passion, of the rising energy of Kundalini—chi unbounded—set free to spiral and forever reach for new horizons. It is the driving inspiration of evolution, the engine that moves us, the fire that consumes the flesh of material existence. Without *Eros* science and humanity has no soul, it has no inspired vision, no source of story for its mythos and its worldview. *Eros* has no methodology and this is why it is the vehicle of our dreams and the voice of dreamers. But in order for dreams to become reality, in order for *Eros* to continue to burn so brightly, it needs a constant source of fuel: *Logos* or reason. *Logos* provides structure. *Logos* provides a method for implementing the eternal dream of *Eros*. *Logos* is the discernment and the distillation of *Eros*'s eternal vision.

As noted earlier the practitioner of experiential shamanism who has made the journey into nonordinary states of consciousness comes to know the world through *Eros*, yet that same practitioner also knows that upon returning to our ordinary state of consciousness *Logos* is a vital necessity. This is because in order to implement *Eros*'s vision, spirit must come back down into the body. It must re-inhabit the earth; it must descend from the mountain and unfold its vision through community and the actual rebirth of new life. Shamanism becomes an example of the union between *Eros* and *Logos;* while the shaman becomes the walker between two epistemological worlds that are intimately connected, but which have been progressively disconnected.

Logos is the voice of science and in many respects also of religion, which is currently based solely on our knowledge of ordinary states of consciousness. And as such *Logos* is incomplete without *Eros*. Each needs the other for completeness. *Eros* and *Logos* are like two sides of a coin, mirror opposites that need each other to sustain their mutual existence. *Logos* provides the pattern of the continually weaving loom of life, while *Eros* provides the *theoria*, the theater of the mind, whose vision continually carries us forward. *Restoration Earth* seeks to mirror the shaman, journeying through, making sense of, and resolving challenges of a complex world guided by a unified epistemology of the grounding *Logos* and the inspiring *Eros*.

Freeing Ourselves from Modernity's Existential Crisis
to Find Hope in Contemporary Culture

Western society in particular lives in a state of contradictory experience in the unfolding 21st century. On one hand we are and have been facing overwhelming feelings of hopelessness ranging from rising unemployment to the constant and barely imaginable threat of the eco-crisis. On the other, we defend against our hopelessness with an infallible and blind optimism of hope springing eternal with little action required on our own individual parts. This conflicted state may be readily seen in Nik Turner's (1994) poem, "Watching the Grass Grow", which reads:

> We are the Survivors
> The eternal survivors
> Androgynous energies
> Travelling through time
>
> Particle Accelerators
> Morality Degenerators
> Dadata Disseminators
> Cyclotron Attenuators
> Hyperspatial Conflagrators
>
> Well your neutron bomb neutralised your history

Wiped cancer from the Earth, and mystery
Now we're pushing over concrete
Blowing up the rockery
Watching the garden
Letting the grass grow

We all know where the flowers went today
Media explosion blew them all away
After the thunder
Always comes the rain
We're coming up again
Letting the grass grow

Post future reality, it's a better real world
Post future reality, it's a real better world
Post future super-reality, it's a real super world
Post holocaust hilarity, it's a super real world
Post future surreality, it's sure a surreal world
Post future surreality, it's a real surreal world

Tell me Doc Spock have you got all your answers
Ephemeral vision recalling the dancers

But will we survive?
We always do
We're coming up again
Watching the grass grow.

Negotiating this despair and optimism we may turn towards Sartre to help us define how we live in two seemingly contradictory states. Sartre (1996/2007) argued the nature of reality was that of pure subjectivity defined by individual choices each person makes. Through the act of "choosing to be this or that" (p. 24) we are ultimately making a statement of value—and that statement of value is always seen as good; we are always making the "good" choice. And this choice, in Sartre's understanding of reality, was a choice that would ultimately commit every other human being to it. In short, the choice of one would reverberate to the whole or as Sartre writes: we become "a legislator choosing at the same time what humanity as a whole should be" (p. 25). To Sartre the responsibility of choice for self and other—for determining the value of choices—created three unbearable psychological crises: anguish (the emotional response to having to make a choice that impacts others), abandonment (at the recognition no other will choose for oneself), and despair (a recognition of probability in life—that is of being unable to predict the outcome before the choice). In Sartre's conceptualization, our worldviews are our collective patterns of choices that we have ascribed a value (a degree of goodness or rightness) to and reinforce through our everyday engagements with others. To make a different decision means to consciously encounter the recognition that one's prior choices are no longer "valuable"—and with this a crisis of self and Other. To Sartre, the challenge to ultimately address these defended against emotional states was to fully realize them and one's responsibility to the whole—one's creative power in determining the direction of the human community.

Sartre's (1948) illustration of the existential significance of choice in our lives may be most visibly depicted in his play *No Exit* and the interrelationship of three people who have been condemned to Hell as a consequence of their actions. Begging for a release from his torment, Joseph Garcin cries out:

> Open the door! Open, blast you! I'll endure anything, your red-hot tongs and molten lead, your racks
> and prongs, and garrotes—all your fiendish gadgets, everything that burns and flays and tears—I'll put
> up with any torture you impose. Anything, anything would be better than this agony of mind, this

creeping pain that gnaws and fumbles and caresses one and never hurts enough. [He grips the door-knob and rattles it.] Now will you open? [The door flies open with a jerk, and he just avoids falling.] Ah! [A long silence.] . . . [meditatively]: Now I wonder why that door opened. (Sartre, p. 42–43)

Garcin is a coward and this is why he has been condemned; that is, Garcin has been condemned to Hell because he has failed to examine and internalize the shadow side of his personality. Instead of walking through the door into the unknown, thereby facing his collective shadow (which would liberate him from his suffering), Garcin chooses to put up with the torture of his agony of mind, remaining in the comforting familiarity of his cell. It is this same cowardice, reinforced by our dissociation from intuitive insight (our *cultural amnesia* [see p. 51, this issue, for a definition]) that has held the modern mind prisoner within the limits of our contemporary epistemological frameworks.

Still there is another part of Garcin that seeks personal reflection and wants to internalize the collective shadow. He wants to "set his life in order" (Sartre, 1948, p. 13). But he is prevented from participating in this process of personal reflection, and therefore further condemned, due to the actions of the other two members of this play, Inez Serrano and Estelle Rigault. Inez is a lesbian who wants to have a love affair with Estelle. Estelle, on the other hand, is a nymphomaniac who wants to have Garcin as her lover. Estelle offers herself as a gift of healing to Garcin, whose acceptance will help to soothe his torment. The irony of their situation is Garcin wants nothing else than to be left alone so that he can ponder his own thoughts; while everything Estelle does is a means to gain the attention of Garcin. Estelle thereby represents the personification of humankind's socially constructed consumer culture—*Eros* spurned, substituted, and transformed into ugliness—with its emphasis on what Erich Fromm (1947) has referred to as the *marketing orientation*. According to Fromm, "The character orientation which is rooted in the experience of oneself as a commodity and of one's value as exchange value I call *the marketing orientation* [italics added]" (p. 68). Inez—like the modern mind—remains trapped in her state of Hell by becoming consumed with her *Logos*-oriented rational analysis of why the three of them have been placed together in this situation, all the while wanting an experiential encounter with *Eros*, as she tries desperately to win over the erotic feelings of Estelle so that they can become lovers. In these characters, Sartre's play *No Exit* thus represents humankind's failure to examine its personal and collective shadow, the choices that contribute to this failure, and the outcomes of operating from a pure *Eros* or a pure *Logos* epistemology.

Garcin represents those parts of us that both fear examining our personal shadow and are continually prevented from beginning the process of examination by the effects of the collective shadow and the collective choices, which are represented by the actions of Estelle and Inez. Sartre's (1948) insight into understanding the problem of evil in the world can therefore be summed up by saying that Hell is not an ontological domain, but is instead a psychological state. Heaven (or what is good) then is a psychological state, whose actualization within us is continually thwarted because of humankind's failure to examine our personal and collective shadow—as seen depicted in the opening poem of this section, whereby the seemingly horrific components of human life are repackaged into a shallow optimism that ultimately prohibits us from confronting our choices and making new ones to establish the possibility of a truly healthier and sustainable world. In effect, our fear of confronting the diminished value of our prior choices and the shadow elements of our nature, we in turn perpetuate the crises that create our anguish.

Another way to look at Sartre's (1948) insights is to explore the Hindu game of *Maya*, the game of illusion or the game of hide-and-seek (Watts, 1972). In other words, *No Exit* is a play that symbolizes humankind's search for our primordial state of "transpersonal ecosophical wholeness." Whereby the psychological labyrinth of *Maya* can be understood as the product of our rational formation of ego (or self-consciousness) which has created the illusion that our mind and body are separate, that we are separate from one another and that humankind is separate from the world of nature. Hindus believe that we remain in this state of confusion about who we are, chained to the great wheel of birth and death, until we are able to free ourselves from *Maya* (from our state of Hell) and fully integrate the shadow elements of our unconscious into a transpersonal orientation of cosmos and consciousness (Metzner, 1996, 1998); that is unifying *Eros* and *Logos*.

Richard Tarnas (1991) discusses this ongoing struggle of humankind's attempt to reach self-awareness in his book *The Passion of the Western Mind*, explaining that Sartre's *No Exit* also deals with the existentialist dilemma that our potential for self-actualization is perceived as nothing more than a purely secular process of growth: that the potential for self-transcendence is bounded by "a priori metaphysical limits" (p. 406), a rationally conceived theoretical threshold which serves to hold us prisoner within the private (self-contained) and isolated (atomistic) confines of our "skin-encapsulated egos" (Watts, 1961, p. 23). This is why philosopher Immanuel Kant believed that humankind is bound to its social construction of reality, and why, as a consequence, we are unable to have any direct experience of the *numinous* and/or the transpersonal.

The stark reality of this dilemma invites us to ask: Is there no way of setting ourselves free of the modern mind's epistemological limits? Are we doomed to living an existence that is void of the passionate caress of *Eros*? Are we never to know again the true power of erotic sensuality and love that can only be experienced subjectively as we struggle to free ourselves from the modern mind's lonely objective existence through virtual reality and even more elaborate technologized con-games of *Logos*? Are we never to be liberated from the cognitive habits of our social conditioning? Abraham Maslow and those who have taken up his investigations into the farther reaches of human nature believe there is. And it is here, in the drive to merge *Eros* and *Logos*; to free ourselves to make choices without fears of despair, abandonment, and anguish; to locate a sincere optimism in the future precisely because we are consciously dealing with the crises of the present rather than denying them, that *Restoration Earth* has emerged.

Stepping Off: Beginning the Fool's Journey[5]

First steps are challenging and terrifying. It is no wonder that Sartre (1996/2007) identified the act of choice itself as one that carries with it anguish. One inevitably questions whether the path one is choosing is correct; one wonders if one has everything they need. And the list goes on from there. This is the first issue of *Restoration Earth* (which we have nicknamed *RE* for short) and it is the first step in the path towards answering our above challenges. In this first issue we have attempted to gather literature from a diverse array of disciplines to highlight the range of perspectives looking at our current global society, our crises, and the possibility of reconciliation—within ourselves, between our human relations, between ourselves and the Natural world, and to our history. We have attempted to illustrate what it might look like to have both *Eros* and *Logos* expressed in a unified whole. In so doing we begin the journal featuring a previously unpublished piece by Arne Naess, the ecophilosopher who has inspired both of us (Mark and Katie) in our own intellectual, spiritual, and social journeys that brought us to founding this journal.

In this article, we hear Naess's familiar voice critiquing the *how* we are talking about and conceptualizing the eco-crisis. He writes emphatically that how we talk (or write) about the eco-crisis shapes how we think about it and ultimately what we do. He suggests that calling it an environmental crisis obscures it and keeps it dislocated from us; he reminds us we are "clearly *inside* the ecological system of Earth" (p. 14). And he reminds us that the future health of Earth and all of its species depends upon the embrace of cultural diversity. He reinforces his principle ecosophical belief in the intrinsic value of Earth, all its diverse species, and the rich array of diversity in human communities.

Following Naess, Alan Drengson, a close friend and colleague of Naess and an essential contributor to the development of the deep ecology movement, tells us the story of environmental studies through his own personal experience. Providing the reader with a glimpse of the historical contexts that allowed a transformation of consciousness to emerge within Western civilization that there was, in fact, a serious problem

---

[5] The Fool is a traditional archetypal figure who will transform into a hero/heroine through the arduous task of living a life with unknown outcomes. The Fool engages in the brave act of being willing to make a choice to move from as, Noble (1983/1994), writes "the void, the precreation state containing all possibilities but not yet manifesting any particular things" (p. 23). Further Noble, citing Jungian analyst Marie Louise von Franz, writes "the Fool is a glyph of 'psychic wholeness. . . . before the rise of ego consciousness, or any kind of dividing consciousness'" (p. 23).

emerging on a planetary scale, we see how one individual incorporated this information to respond. Drengson does not illustrate a human being awash in anguish, abandonment, and despair in choosing to act. Instead, Drengson demonstrates one may act and sustain this forward momentum for change, even while recognizing the journey itself is far longer than one individual lifetime and unpredictable. Drengson highlights the communal nature of a consciousness shift and the decision to act. We may never share a universal theistic belief to comfort all of us so that we may not feel utterly abandoned and alone; but Drengson illustrates that the communal nature of acting towards halting (and potentially reversing) the eco-crisis links us to others both immediately and in the future. In short, through collective action towards promoting care of the Earth we suddenly find ourselves in a community—we come home to a place where we are secure.

It is within the theme of home and homecoming that we locate Florence Shepard's article. Exploring the multilayered meaning of home, Shepard shares of her own personal journey searching for home. She explores home as a location that exists in our psychological, relational, cultural, physical, and natural places, each with their own distinct meanings and each with their sources of benefit in helping us find our place in the world. She openly writes about the challenges of Western definitions of home and how these often leave women, including herself, feeling conflicted—an echo of what we describe in this introduction of the dislocation of women to secondary status in a *Logos*-oriented worldview. Yet her story is one in which we may redefine the definitions and we may ultimately shed ourselves from beliefs that confine us. We see Shepard's exploration further distilled through Vidya Sarveswaran's commentary, where she extends the discussion into bioregional theory, specifically the Indian concept *tinai* and explores how a bioregional perspective of home may function to promote an egalitarian society.

We move from personal reflections on our current crisis to alternative perspectives on *how* we arrived here and *what* may inspire us to adopt a new state of consciousness, a new paradigm that will allow us to collectively act to promote the well-being and realization of all species on earth. How might we increase the probability that the outcome of our species is a sustainable, equitable, and just society? We begin this exploration with a speculative piece on how we arrived at this crisis in the first place from an evolutionary perspective. Evolutionary biologist and Taoist, Michael Caley explores, in his article "The Pooh Hypothesis: A Response", the concept of neoteny and its application to human society. He asks us whether we have domesticated ourselves through thousands of years so that we are, in effect, adolescents attempting to problem-solve our way out of a situation we simply do not have the developmental abilities to address. He suggests we are a species in search of our elders to help guide us and teach us how to direct our impulsive energy.

And where to find guidance is precisely what Mark A. Schroll explores in his article "Sufi Wisdom, Norse Mythology, Zen Koans, and the Eco-Crisis: Remembering the Value of Teaching-Stories". Schroll examines the rich heritage of our myths and teaching stories as possible elders providing us wisdom for a shift in consciousness. Through engaging with and creating new stories, we have the possibility of changing the human narratives that keep us repeating cycles of behavior that have brought us to and keep us at the brink of ecological disaster. Schroll highlights how myths and storytelling remain embedded components of shamanistic cultures and are at the core of our pre-technological heritage. They have the capacity to remind us of our interdependency (and our elders)—both upon each other and the planet.

In Jorge Conesa-Sevilla's article we encounter the possibility of the very emergence of our aesthetic mind as being intimately linked to Nature, specifically one tree, *Acacia tortillis*. Conesa-Sevilla explores our earliest evolutionary cultural heritage from our earliest *Homo erectus* ancestors through the emergence of Western Monotheism and our relationship to the trees within this genus. He suggests that we may not have emerged endowed with all of our unique abilities that define us if it were not for our intimate relationship with a tree.

Simon Ralli Robinson develops the discussion on the possibilities of relationships to plants and the development of new states of consciousness in his own personal story of shamanic initiation and his experience with *ayahuasca*, a drink utilized in several South American indigenous spiritual practices to enable individuals to alter their consciousness to aid them in their life or the lives of members of their community.

15

Robinson provides us a vivid example of what we discussed in this introduction on how shamanism provides a unified experience between *Eros* and *Logos*.

Following Robinson, we conclude our group of articles exploring why and how and begin to examine *what do we do* and *how do we do it*. When we know we need to change; when we know we have identified the problem; when we have sufficiently shifted our consciousness: what do we do with all of our awakened knowledge? Here we encounter Mark A. Schroll's second piece "Vision Quest—Awakening Transpersonal Ecosophy: Practical Solutions Toward a Sustainable Culture". Not only does Schroll articulate what a transpersonal ecosophy is, which is the underlying philosophical orientation of *RE*, but more specifically he explores through his own personal experience how a change in consciousness may lead to a change in behavior—specifically when we change our awareness of the natural world from an object to full beingness with "dignity" (as Naess might say [1976/1989]) we are suddenly compelled to *act* differently. When our underlying state of consciousness (or paradigm) changes, we change and we become open to new possibilities that a life embedded *inside* Nature (as Naess reminds us in our first article) may provide us with a healthier life.

And this brings us to the essays by Mark Glasgow and Meredith Ball. Ball introduces the reader to a mode of therapy known as *Horticultural Therapy*, whereby individuals engage in activities such as gardening for therapeutic purposes. She discusses the practice of this intervention and the research that has demonstrated its widespread success in promoting a higher quality of life and improved mental health for a range of populations. While Glasgow provides the reader with a qualitative study on the use of the specific therapeutic intervention Natural Systems Thinking Process developed by Michael Cohen in changing a person's perception of connectedness to nature and also in ameliorating feelings of despair and anxiety associated with our modern, Nature-disconnected life.

At which point our journal turns its focus on new books presenting new ideas and ways of seeing the eco-crisis and how we address it. Molly Remer explores Ellen LaConte's new work *Life Rules*, exploring a dramatic and shocking new metaphor for the eco-crisis in an attempt to generate a shift in consciousness—to propel individuals into seeing it with new eyes; while Tanya Collings explores Alan Drengson's text *Wild Way Home* and its exploration of a life orientation that promotes an intimate relationship to Nature and thus a capacity of care.

Our journal concludes with a short story by writer and playwright Lynne Elson entitled "Letting Go," while not giving away the plot, Elson creates an example of art whereby the presence of Nature and other species remind the protagonist that she is not abandoned. You will also find throughout the journal poems and photography by poet Anne Westlund that explore her experience engaging with the Natural world in her own home area of Washington state (her brother has also contributed photographs reminding us that we first come to see the world with our families), as well as a poem by Turkish writer and poet Evin Okçuoğlu that explores the relationship between social justice and nature.

And with these diverse pieces, we begin our Fool's journey where we attempt to increase the probability that humanity *can* co-create a new sustainable future; where we recognize Nature *is* home and we are not, nor can ever be abandoned. We hope that you enjoy and venture forward with us!

References

Berry, T. (1988). *The dream of the earth*. San Francisco, CA: Sierra Club Books.

Bohm, D. & Peat, F. D. (1987). *Science, order, and creativity*. New York: Bantam Books.

Carse, J. P. (1986). *Finite and infinite games*. New York: Ballantine Books.

Davies, P. (1983). *God and the new physics*. New York: Simon & Schuster, Inc.

Diamond, J. (1991). Drowning dogs and the dawn of art. *Natural History, 102*, 22–29.

Eliade, M. (1964). *Shamanism: Archaic techniques of ecstasy* (W.R. Trask, trans.). Princeton, NJ: Princeton University Press. (Original publication 1951)

Feinstein, D., & Krippner, S. (1988). *Personal mythology: Using ritual, dreams, and imagination to discover your inner story*. Los Angeles: Jeremy P. Tarcher, Inc.

Fromm, E. (1947). *Man for himself: An inquiry into the psychology of ethics*. New York: Rinehart and Company, Inc.

Gribbin, J. (1986). *In search of the big bang: Quantum physics and cosmology*. New York: Bantam Books.

Griffin, D. R. (1988). Introduction: The reenchantment of science. In D. R. Griffin (Ed.), *The reenchantment of science: Postmodern proposals*, (pp. 1–46). Albany, NY: State University of New York Press.

Harvey, G. (Ed.). (2003). *Shamanism: A reader*. New York: Routledge.

Hillman, J., & Ventura, M. (1992). *We've had a hundred years of psychotherapy and the world's getting worse*. San Francisco: HarperSanFrancisco.

Jeans, Sir J. (1981). *Physics and philosophy*. New York: Dover Publications. (Original publication 1943)

Krippner, S. (2002). Conflicting perspectives on shamans and shamanism: Points and counterpoints. *American Psychologist, 57*(11), 962–977.

Lakoff, G., & Johnson, M. (1980). *Metaphors we live by*. Chicago, IL: The University of Chicago Press.

Meeker, J. (1997). *The comedy of survival: Literary ecology and a play ethic*. Tuscon, AZ: University of Arizona Press.

Metzner, R. (1996). The Buddhist six-worlds model of consciousness and reality. *The Journal of Transpersonal Psychology, 28* (2), 155–166.

Metzner, R. (1998). *The unfolding self: Varieties of transformative experience*. Novato, CA: Origin Press.

Metzner, R. (1999). *Green psychology: Transforming our relationship to the earth*. Rochester, VT: Park Street Press.

Naess, A. (1989). *Ecology, community and lifestyle: Outline of an ecosophy* (D. Rothenberg, trans.). New York: Cambridge University Press. (Original publication 1976)

Noble, V. (1994). *Motherpeace: A way to the Goddess through myth, art, and tarot*. New York: HarperCollins Publishers. (Original publication 1983)

Parrinder, G. (1985). *World religions: From ancient history to the present*. New York: Facts on File, Inc.

Prigogine, I., & Stengers, I. (1984). *Order out of chaos: Man's new dialogue with nature*. New York: Bantam Books.

Sartre, J-P. (1948). *No exit and three other plays*. New York: Vintage Books.

Sartre, J-P. (2007). *Existentialism is humanism* (C. Macomber, trans.). New Haven, Conn: Yale University Press. (Original publication 1996)

Schroll, M. A. (2011). Neo-shamanism, psi, and their relationship with transpersonal psychology. *Paranthropology: Journal of Anthropological Approaches to the Paranormal, 2*(4), 26–36.

Schroll, M. A. & Walker, H. (2011). Diagnosing the human superiority complex: Providing evidence the eco-crisis is born of conscious agency. *Anthropology of Consciousness, 22*(1), 39-48.

Schroll, M. A. & Greenwood, S. (2011). Worldviews in collision/worldviews in metamorphosis: Toward a multistate paradigm. *Anthropology of Consciousness, 22*(1), 49–60.

Singer, J. (1990). *Seeing through the visible world: Jung, gnosis, and chaos*. San Francisco: Harper & Row, Publishers.

Tarnas, R. (1991). *The passion of the Western mind: Understanding the ideas that have shaped our worldview*. New York: Ballantine Books.

Tart, C. T. (1975). Science, states of consciousness, and spiritual experiences: The need for state-specific sciences. In C. T. Tart (Ed.), *Transpersonal psychologies* (pp. 11–58). New York: Harper & Row Publishers.

Thom, R. (1975). *Structural stability and morphogenesis*. Reading, MA: Benjamin.

Toulmin, S. (1982). *The return of cosmology: Postmodern science and the theology of nature*. Berkeley, CA: University of California Press.

Turner, N. (1994). Watching the grass grow. *Prophets of time*. Los Angeles, CA: Cleopatra.

Vitebsky, P. (2001). *The shaman: Voyages of the soul, trance, ecstasy and healing from Siberia to the Amazon*. London: Duncan Baird Publishers.

Watts, A. W. (1972). *The book: On the taboo against knowing who you are*. New York: Vintage Books.

Weber, R. (1986). The search for unity. In R. Weber (Ed.), *Dialogues with saints and sages: The search for unity* (pp. 1-19). London: Routledge & Kegan Paul.

Wright, R. (2009). *The evolution of God*. New York: Little, Brown, and Company.

Yunt, J. D. (2001). Jung's contribution to an ecological psychology. *Journal of Humanistic Psychology, 41*(2), 96–121.

※※※

KATHERINE E. BATTEN (MACDOWELL), D.Th., is the founder and dean of Ocean Seminary College, a tuition- and barrier- free interreligious graduate school designed to promote the reconnection of nature and science to religious studies and practice. She is the author of several publications in journals, magazines, and textbooks. Most recently she contributed an autobiographical piece to *SageWoman* magazine (2011 issue *Healing Ourselves*) about the woman's shamanic tradition she teaches and practices known as Pillar Seiðr (say-ther). She holds an interreligious ordination and is also ordained as a Summoner by Z. Budapest within the Dianic Goddess tradition and serves on the board of the Institute for Thealogy and Deasophy. She holds multiple graduate degrees in addition to her doctorate in theology, including masters degrees in comparative religious studies, Christian history, Buddhism, counseling psychology and is a doctoral candidate in health and clinical psychology. She has spent 8 years working as a clinical therapist specializing in addictions, trauma, and personality disorders.

In addition to her academic work, Katie is a published poet of five volumes of poetry: *Witness, Vestiges & Bones, Turning the Silver Wheel, Into Quiet,* and *Love Amongst the Fishes,* and her nature photography was recently collected and published under the title *A Study of Sandy Hook.* She is a professional singer and composer and has multiple recordings including: *My Name Is…, Hitchhiker, 9 Sacred Pillars* (for orchestra), *Chasing Zebras* (sonatas for guitar and piano), and *Son of Arianrhod* (sonatas or cello and piano); as well as a compilation of her vocal work *She Waits: A Retrospective.* She is an award-winning playwright and is currently at work on her symphony *Threnody for Earth,* an excerpt of which was recorded and released on her compilation album. She shares her life with her closest friend, a cocker spaniel named Charlotte; several rambunctious turtles, sea stars, shrimps, clownfish and seahorses (and some very interesting snails and a sneaky gobi named "Randall"); and her tribe of human friends, family, and loved ones. Contact: oceanseminary@verizon.net

MARK A. SCHROLL, Ph.D., Research Adjunct Faculty, Institute of Transpersonal Psychology, Palo Alto, California, and serves on the Advisory Board of *Alternative Therapies in Health and Medicine.* He served as Guest Managing Editor of the special *Anthropology of Consciousness, 22*(1), 2011 issue "From Primordial Anthropology to a Transpersonal Ecosophy", and *Anthropology of Consciousness, 16*(1), 2005 issue "Primordial Visions in an Age of Technology". He co-chaired the 2009 "Bridging Nature and Human Nature" annual Society for the Anthropology of Consciousness conference co-sponsored by the Association for Transpersonal Psychology. He serves on the Editorial Board of *Paranthropology: Journal of Anthropological Approaches to the Paranormal.* He serves on the Windbridge Institute Scientific Advisory Board. He was the Founding Editor of *Rhine Online: Psi-News Magazine.* He Edited *Rhine Online, 3*(1), 2011, the special 2nd-anniversary issue "Sacred Sites, Consciousness, and the Eco-Crisis". He serves on the Editorial Board of *Goddess Thealogy: An International Journal for the Study of Feminism and Religion* and the Board of the Institute for Thealogy and Deasophy. He has been invited to serve as the Co-Editor of the 1st issue of *Goddess Thealogy* with Patricia 'Iolana (In Press). Schroll is a transpersonal cultural theorist and conference organizer with multi-disciplinary interests ranging from philosophy of science to transpersonal ecosophy. Contact: rockphd4@yahoo.com

Cultural Diversity, Ecological Crisis and Decreasing Unsustainability

Arne Naess

Naess, A. (2011). Cultural diversity, ecological crisis and decreasing unsustainability. *Restoration Earth: An Interdisciplinary Journal for the Study of Nature & Civilization, 1*(1), 19–23. Copyright © The Authors. All rights reserved. For reprint information contact: oceanseminary@verizon.net.

I will discuss certain relations between culture and the global process of increasing ecological unsustainability. One of the many factors which make it difficult to change the process into one of decreasing unsustainability is the shift in ways of thinking to that of ecology from that of environment. The latter term suggests that we have to do with something *outside* humanity, something we regrettably are dependent upon. It is easier to mobilize people and money if we acknowledge the human tendency for self-destruction, through policies and actions that spoil our nests, and lead away from our basic goals in life, whether or not it is called happiness. The increasing ecological unsustainability is much nearer to our souls and selves than we have traditionally assumed.

It is often acknowledged that overcoming the increasing ecological crisis—the still increasing level of ecological unsustainability—leads invariably to problems in the humanities, sociology and political sciences. It even fosters new branches like "environmental diplomacy". The Canadian government decided to propose to stop complaining harshly about air pollution in Canada due to US pollutants *provided* the government of the US agreed to a trade treaty favourable to Canada.

It is accepted today that every major ecological problem has a social *and* political aspect. Furthermore, it is clear that technological invention, even of a revolutionary kind since the 60s, such as solar energy, had practically no influence on the curve of increasing unsustainability. Whether the use of an ecologically salutary invention is adopted on an appropriate scale depends upon social and political factors. Unfortunately these factors are neglected in R&D (research and development) programs. Natural science has a higher cultural standing, and governments now gladly spend money on studies of climate, the ozone layer, and similar unpolitical issues.

Turning the attention to the situation in the Third and Fourth Worlds, old stable cultural traditions have played, and still play, a decisive role. Among such traditions we often find ecologically sophisticated and beneficial technologies and ways of life. The influence of industrial societies, including that of mass tourism, has increased in strength in this century, and it has with few exceptions been negative.

An example: The traditional Sherpa culture in Nepal has strict rules regarding how to make use of trees and bushes for heating. Living between 2000 and 4000 meters in the Himalayas with long cold winters, the vital need was clear. Thus only dead trees were used. With tourism the Sherpas got jobs, especially as mountain guides and porters. Their mobility increased immensely. There was, to use an expression about development in ECU, an "avalanche" of transport across traditional borders.

The ethics and practice in relation to forests and vegetation in general had been local in the sense of protection of natural resources locally, not a more general concern. So, as soon as the Sherpas were far from home, they would cut and burn everything, for instance, in order to secure hot showers for tourists every morning.

In short, wonderful ecological ethics and practices in many non-industrial countries had often or mostly local areas of *validity and dominance*. It turned out that the tourists' *way of life* generally was conceived as one with very little ethical and other constraints, and yet nevertheless capable of securing a fabulously high material standard of living. Large scale corruption has been a regular consequence—with a few notable exceptions.

A very important development since the 60s has been the emergence of a drive among people in the

Western industrial nations to join minorities in the Third and Fourth Worlds to re-establish ecologically sane technologies and ways of life. One group called "social ecologists" comprises a subgroup, for instance in Uruguay, living and working among the "poor" to support the few, mostly very old people, who still remember and make use of those technologies.

The introduction of Western, mostly unecological, technology has mostly a devastating influence on *culture* and upon the state of the economy, for instance, requiring imports and "help," and increasing the distance between rich and poor. (For example, the influence of the so-called "green revolution" based on Western agricultural technology.)

Unfortunately the cooperation of Westerners who are competent to work in the spirit of the above-mentioned subgroup of social ecologists, is not favored by Western colleges and universities. Effective cooperation with the "poor" people requires, not only knowledge of cultural anthropology and ability to live a life in a foreign country that is not provocative and strange, but also a willingness to stay there for years. And Westerners should be fairly sure that when they come back to their own countries they are either able to find a job, or are helped to train for available kinds of jobs.

If the devastating ecological trend in the Third and Fourth Worlds is going to be changed, it is necessary that the institutions in the West understand their responsibility either to decrease Western pernicious influence or to change it into a beneficial one.

Every year counts. To teach environmental ethics, as it is now accepted at many Western colleges and universities, is a very indirect help, especially because it is mostly "meta-ethics", that is, academic discussions about various theories *about* ethics. Even in academic institutions ethics was what is now called "normative ethics" prescribing (and discussing) duties, obligations in various sorts of life situations, and wise guidelines. Also, of course, discussing consequences and evaluating guidelines in the light of consequences.

One of the reasons governments in many industrial countries now finance environmental, academic ethics may be that it costs so much less than studies centring on social and political means to fight the ecological crisis, and much less than doing—on a proper scale—anything about it. One may compare this to the 50 years from 1830 to 1880, when there was much *talk* about the misery of labour. Women in the aristocracy weaved and sewed clothing for the poor; there were constant fund-raisings to help the poor, but on a scale that was completely insufficient. As with now, economics was used as an explanation: more wealth among the wealthy must be accumulated in order to change conditions for the poor in a decisive way.

There are today two different basic attitudes towards non-human beings. According to the so-called "anthropocentric attitude," no non-human being can have value in itself. It can only have instrumental value, that is, value as a means for humans. Among contemporary philosophers, Habermas expressed such a view. The other basic attitude of Bill Devall and Gary Snyder for instance, holds that non-humans may have value in themselves independent of what they can be for humans.

As long as there were a moderate number of humans with moderate means to interfere with the richness and diversity of life on Earth, it did not matter much for the planet how they conceived their relation to the Earth. But now, with an enormous number of people, and a practically infinite capacity for destruction, how they feel about nature is of great importance. The simplest reason for this is ignorance of the long-range effects of their interferences. A so-called "green society" is expected to be ecologically sustainable. The term is mostly also used in such a way that a society deserves the name only if also the peace and the distribution problems are largely solved.

There is unfortunately a tendency to talk about the "environmental" crisis rather than the "ecological" crisis. "Environment" is conceived as something *outside* of humanity. Humans are clearly *inside* the ecological systems of the Earth. The societies of humans have the same *kind* of need and right to be protected as societies of other living beings. The rapid extinction of non-industrial societies is ecosystem degradation and destruction. The threat of the extinction of cultures has an ethical aspect, and it belongs to the proper problematics of general ecology: *Protection of human cultural diversity is a genuine part of the protection of biodiversity.*

Writers who characterize a (future) *green society* sometimes make it clear that they describe a utopia, others intend to describe a future society which will be a reality, if the ecological crisis is overcome.

There is, in my view, a regrettable tendency to talk and write about *green societies* as if they will be realizations of only one culture. In my opinion, the absence of deeply different future cultures would be a calamity. *Richness and diversity of future cultures is for me a great ideal*, perhaps the only way towards further developments of the human species. Diversity of subcultures, as we see them today for instance in big cities, cannot replace diversity of cultures. In at least a couple of decades there were thousands of new musicians in a certain part of New York City—thousands who lived "in and for music". As long as the children were exposed to very different lifestyles and value systems, no *specific culture* was created. No traditions, no completeness.

Most pictures of conditions in a green society suggest a rather uniform way of life. I reckon that some people will relish conspicuous consumption. Some will be victims of unsatisfied greed; some will delight in ecologically expensive gadgets. But in the latter case, the owners of these gadgets will have to live ecologically, that is using other ecologically inexpensive ways to meet their needs. The laws or mores should tolerate great differences of lifestyles. Today we know how some people may spend 90% of their income for purposes for which others would not even spend 5%.

The protection of richness and diversity of life forms is compatible with a variety of political systems. But national socialist and fascist systems are intolerant of deep cultural diversity and therefore cannot furnish the basis for green societies. There is a great literature comparing communism, socialism and capitalism. Also "vertical" versus "horizontal" societies are compared, and "tightness" versus "looseness". As long as only vague descriptions of countries are offered for comparison, next to nothing can be concluded about their relative merits on the way to ecological sustainability.

The presumption among most writers is that democracies are "best." The argumentation is weak because it mostly relies on historical and contemporary evidence, that is, on an actual ecological state of affairs. Authoritarian, hierarchical, Buddhist countries have often been used as examples of countries with great chances of remaining ecologically responsible in spite of not being democracies, but they are not industrial societies. If the democracies of the West do not within x years, for instance 50 years, change their ecological policies in the direction of decreasing unsustainability, the catastrophic situation may be reached when "strongmen" are able to acquire power and change policies by decrees. My guess is that ecological dictatorships have no better chance to be realized than "ecological democracy".

One may ask what is the relation between the various *existing* forms of "systems" of economy, technology, family relations, reproduction habits, religion, and so on, and the relative prospects leading to ecological sustainability? The answers are in many ways hypothetical, because it is difficult to say to what degree a deplorable or less deplorable situation of a country is due to the "system". The so-called "systems" are changing all the time, even in the cultures called "traditional." One cannot easily predict how a worsening ecological crisis will be met. People read that because of our irresponsible behaviour, we may cause a new ice age or a meter high rise of the water level of the ocean—even within less than *a hundred* years—and many get concerned. They approve appropriate measures to be taken. But when they read what might be the effect of the continued "population explosion," they often are reluctant to approve ethically acceptable, appropriate measures. There are or have recently been cultures with norms favourable to the stability of population size.

Among animals, biological processes that limit reproduction are fairly common when resources are small or dwindling. For example, there are insects which every autumn, when "anticipating" winter and spring time scarcity, produce fewer females. Resources on remote islands are in an obvious way limited and this has motivated appropriate customs. Malthus thought that Norway's agricultural population had customs that counteracted the blind drive for procreation. One the whole, cultures today do not have institutions favourable for early *stabilization and reduction* of population.

The small minority of 500 million who are responsible for most of the degradation of life conditions on Earth tolerate cultural patterns today that favour irresponsible reproduction. A 10% decrease in the birth of unwanted children would make richer European countries enter the process of population decrease before long. The increase of criminality among children from age 10 to 15 testifies to the presence of devastating cultural trends which incapacitate adequate education.

21

Many people active in the fight against the ecological crisis look forward to green societies where children from the time they are able to walk have access to patches of *free nature* without crossing dangerous streets. But this requires architectural revolutions. As it is now, *the street* is a cultural centre.

There is, in short, much to be learned from the study of diverse cultures in the past and present, but the global state of affairs is so complex that any fairly simple *general conclusion* about relative merits of different cultures is highly speculative. What we know as members of Western democracies—whatever their cultures—is that we are heavily responsible for *increasing unsustainability*.

The above reflections have as their modest aim emphasizing the importance of increasing efforts in *every* country, under *every* sort of political, cultural etc conditions to "turn the tide," from increasing to decreasing unsustainability.

This conclusion is compatible with a certain mobility of area of concentration: some groups may *concentrate* on overcoming definite dominant ideological or spiritual aspects of their culture (in a wide sense of the word), others may *concentrate* on reforms of the economic systems, still others may *concentrate* on the fight against the implementation of an ecologicaly horrendous concrete plant or some other source of horrible pollution. The frontier for kinds of work is long, and discussions about what is most needed to do should not degrade into polemics.

NB: This essay was written in 1993. It was lightly edited by Alan Drengson in 2010.

ARNE NAESS is a founder of the Deep Ecology Movement. He is one of Norway's best known philosophers and was Professor Emeritus at the University of Oslo. He worked with SUM, a research Institute associated with the University of Oslo from 1991 to his death in 2009. Born in 1912 in Oslo, he graduated from the University of Oslo in 1933. He studied in Paris and Vienna and received his Doctorate in 1936 (thesis title: *Erkenntnis und wissenschaftliches Verhalten*). He was Professor of Philosophy at the University of Oslo from 1939 to 1969, then became a free-lance philosopher and naturalist, and from 1970 onwards an environmental activist. Næss has participated in the peace movement (especially 1940–55) and "the deep ecology movement" (1970 to 2009). He was leader of UNESCO's project on the East/West Controversy (Cold War), Paris 1948–49. In Europe Næss is a supporter of "green" politics. He founded the international periodical *Inquiry*, an interdisciplinary journal devoted to philosophy and the social sciences.

He has lectured in Bali, Beijing, Berkeley, Bucharest, Canada, Canton, Chengdu, Devon, Dubrovnik, Hangzhou, Helsinki, Hongkong, Japan, Jerusalem, London, Melbourne, Reykjavik, Santa Cruz, Taiwan, Tartu (Estonia),Tromsø, Vancouver, Warsaw.

He has received the following Awards:
- Royal Norwegian Order of St. Olav
- Årets Peer Gynt, 2004
- The Nordic Council Award for Nature and Environment, 2002
- Uggla Prize, Humanistiska Föreningen, Stockholm University, 2002
- Diploma & Medal from King Harald V of Norway for his contribution in the Intelligence Agency XU during the German occupation (1998)
- The Medal of the Presidency of the Italian Republic (Italy, 1998)
- The Nordic Prize (Swedish Academy, Sweden, 1996)
- The Mountain Tradition Award (Fjellskikkspris) by the Red Cross, (Oslo, 1996)
- The Mahatma Gandhi Prize for Non-violent Peace (Oslo, 1994)

- Fridtjof Nansens Award (Fridtjof Nansen Foundation for the promotion of Science, 1983)
- The Sonning Prize (Denmark, 1977) for contribution to European culture
- Honorary doctorate Stockholm University (1972)
  The Norwegian National University of Sports and Physical Education (1995)
- Honorary memberships: The Norwegian Alpine Club (2002); The Norwegian Tourist Association (2002)

He has published about 30 books and numerous articles including: *The Selected Works of Arne Naess* (SWAN) 10 volume work (Springer, 2005); *Life's Philosophy: Reason and Feeling in a Deeper World* (2002) (Original title: *Livsfilosofi: Et personlig bidrag om følelser og fornuft*,1998, also in Danish, Swedish, Latvian and English). He led an active life in the outdoors as a mountain climber and skier. He was an internationally respected and widely influential scholar, teacher and writer. Professor Naess died two weeks shy of his 97th birthday in Oslo in January 2009. His wife Kit-Fai carries on his work and is his literary executor. For samples of his work see the 5 issue *Trumpeter* Series in the archives online starting with issues 2005 21, 1 & 2 running through the festschrift of the 2006 22, 1 & 2 issues. See also the paperback anthology of his work *Ecology of Wisdom: Writings by Arne Naess*, edited by Alan Drengson and Bill Devall, published by Counterpoint Press, Emeryville, California in 2010.

"Buck" copyright © 2011 by Chris Westlund. Photo taken in Washington State, USA.

Toprak Su Gibidir
Devrim Kaçınılmaz

Evin Okçuoğlu

Okçuoğlu, E. (2011). Toprak su gibidir devrim kaçınılmaz. *Restoration Earth: An Interdisciplinary Journal for the Study of Nature & Civilization, 1*(1), 24–25.

Okçuoğlu, E. (2011). Revolution is like soil and water it is inevitable (E. Okçuoğlu, trans). *Restoration Earth: An Interdisciplinary Journal for the Study of Nature & Civilization, 1*(1), 24–25.

alın terinden yağmur bulutu birikiyor
güneş kar topluyor karanlık madenlerde
dereler denize dipçik inişinde gürülderken
sınıf kini eritirken demirci
toprağı deşerek biniyorum öfkeme
yüzlerce yılın hırsı kök söküyor tarlada
devrim lavlarına kapılıyor titrek cılız ihanet
puslu sabahı yırtarken sesimiz
parlıyor haykırışımızın gücü
sonsuz devinimin içi sığmıyor içine
insanlık sayfasına ısınıyor içimiz
kaynaşıyor enternasyonal toprakla

Revolution Is Like Soil and Water, It Is Inevitable

Rain cloud is accrued from hard work
sun brings snow from the dark mines
while rivers burble flowing like gunstock down the sea
while smith forges class rancor
I ride on my anger embewolling the soil
hunderds of years' rage grubs in the farm
shaky, puny betrayal is sucked into revolution lavas
while our voice tearing the hazy morning
the power of our scream shines
never ending move is unable to contain itself
we take a shine to the humanity page
knit up the international soil

EVİN OKÇUOĞLU was born in Istanbul, Turkey, in 1956. She graduated Atatürk Training Institute and started teaching English at the high school level. Later she completed 4th year at Marmara University and began work as lecturer at İstanbul University for 19 years. She has written several stories and poems for children, including completing seven books. Additionally, her work for adults has been published in different literature magazines and formally published in 2009. Her second poetry book named *En Guzel Gun Icin* (*For The Most Beautiful Day*) is being published in November 2011. She has translated the book *Kosovalı Kız Zana* (*Girl of Kosovo* by Alice Mead). She has 2 daughters and currently lives in İstanbul.

Names of her books for children are:
Sakın Kızma Anne/Please Don't Get Angry Mom (Nisan, 2006 ATP publising)
Şiir Bahçesi/Poetry Garden (Ekim, 2006 [71 poems for children])
Ünlü Besteciler/Famous Composers (October 2006 [life story of 10 composers])

Çocuk Emeği Öyküleri/ Stories of Working Children (October 2006 [ten stories about working children])
Toprak Öyküleri/ Land Stories, (October 2006 [stories about land])
Konuşan Eşyalar/ Talking Objects (October 2006 [10 Talking Objects stories])
Çilekli Masal Pastası/ Tale Pie Made of Strawberry (October 2007 [10 tales])

For Adults
İçi Görünen Şiirler (Poems 2009)
Sardunya Kırıldıkça (Stories 2009)
En Güzel Gün İçin/ For The Most Beautiful Day (November 2011 [poems])

"Sandy Hook in Winter" copyright © 2010 by Katherine Batten MacDowell. Photo taken in Sandy Hook, New Jersey from *A Study of Sandy Hook* (2011).

Environmental Studies from the Early Years: Impressionistic Reflections

Alan Drengson

Drengson, A. (2011). Environmental studies from the early years: Impressionistic reflections. *Restoration Earth: An Interdisciplinary Journal for the Study of Nature & Civilization, 1*(1), 26–33.

Introduction, Distinctions and Caveats

These are personal reflections on the origins of the Environmental Studies Program at the University of Victoria (UVic). To explain why we started this program, and how it developed, I recount the personal and cultural background of the grass roots environmental movement in the early 1970s. In the 1960s we hardly used the words "environmental movement." This came to refer to efforts in our society to curb widespread damages to farm land, urban environments and the natural world. As environmental concern grew, we distinguished between the environmental movement, environmental studies, environmental education, and applying ecological principles to different disciplines (such as ecopsychology). The science of ecology was identified mainly with biology. An early application of ecological analysis outside biology was in sociology in the 1950s to "urban ecology." We distinguished between educational programs and original research aiming to further knowledge.

In the 1960s several scientific studies showed that human made chemicals are more persistent than we thought, and they can spread through a whole ecosystem. Agricultural chemicals, for example, were found far from their source of application on fields and orchards. In the 1960s the effects of some of these chemicals were implicated in declining reproduction rates of bird species such as bald eagles and brown pelicans. There were well known problems of urban air pollution affecting distant hills, as in the Los Angeles basin. Rachel Carson's book *Silent Spring* (1962) provided an overview of scientific environmental research. We already knew of human damage to the natural world from bad forestry and farming. We were trying to reclaim damaged land and preserve wilderness areas we considered important for the common good. We knew that the 1930s dust bowl years in the Prairies were a result of drought combined with bad agricultural practices.

Public concerns about environmental problems began to grow in the mid-1960s. This led to the first Earth Day in 1970 as people all over the world were eager to support corrective actions. There were deep appraisals of the industrial approach to primary production and energy use. In North America the focused public concern gave rise to the grass roots environmental movement. This was helped by the civil rights and peace movements. By the end of the 1960s grass roots efforts focused on reforming our practices related to war, peace, social justice, and ecological responsibility. There was a proliferation of non-governmental organizations (NGOs). During this time, the academic, scientific, and intellectual communities engaged in sustained environmental research, teaching, and publication. We distinguished between social-political movements such as environmentalism, and programs teaching about relations with nature and environmental responsibility, which we called "environmental education." "Environmental Studies" (ES) referred to programs of interdisciplinary research and education at the post secondary level and including graduate studies. Such programs sought to extend our knowledge beyond narrow specialized foci. We aimed to provide depth *and* comprehensiveness, and to see our society's activities in historical and global contexts.

I will contextualize this social process explaining why we supported educational reforms with new programs of research to study our relations with the natural world. We were changed in ways that enriched our lives and relationships by being professionally and personally engaged in this undertaking. This account is sparse as I only mention some of the many people who were involved in ES on our campus and beyond.

Background and Dawning of Environmental Awareness

The grass roots environmental movement began in North America in the mid 1960s. At the time, there were already conservation-preservation organizations with some national and regional government support for their aims. Many of us grew up aware of the bad effects of poor farming and destructive forestry. We knew treasured places that we wanted to preserve as parks and wilderness areas. Conservation efforts reflected a variety of personal experiences. Some efforts were focused on wildlife species and habitats, others on soils and forests. Commitments were based on what we had learned to value in school, and from adults and our own experiences in nature. We were aware of the history of the conservation-preservation movement in North America. We knew that our aims were part of this larger movement. Our care for the natural world had many historical precedents. We learned from history that such concerns were expressed even in ancient times, for example BCE in Greece and China.

My background is typical of many in this respect. My family lived through the dust bowl years in the prairies. We call these years the "Dirty Thirties." Dad was born on a pioneer homestead. His people were from rural farms in Norway. They knew how to farm carefully to look after the land and its inhabitants. We were taught early to appreciate the natural world *and* good farming. In the Dirty Thirties, major efforts were launched by national and local governments to reclaim damaged land and replant destroyed forests. In school we learned about soil conservation, and how to wisely manage water, soil, and other resources. Our appreciation for the natural world was not limited to cultivated land. It included the wild lands beyond the farms and also the uncultivated stream bottoms. We played on the prairie, in the lakes, rivers and in the wooded groves along the rivers. These were some of our early experiences of human-nature relations, and then the Second World War broke out.

Like many others, our family left the plains around 1941 and went to the West Coast because of the Second World War. As we traveled west on the train, we were awed by the foothills, rivers, forests and mountains of the Rockies and other ranges. On the coast, we were impressed by the beauty of the water, forests, and mountains. In school we met youngsters whose parents took us hiking in the forests and mountains of our area. When we grew older we started climbing and hiking in the wild forests and mountains on our own. For some of us this became a passionate avocation. We loved wild mountain places and considered them sacred. Engaged in these activities as young adults, we met others who shared our love for wild places. We realized that the cities and towns were slowly encroaching on these "sacred" areas. The forests were being clear-cut and replaced by tree plantations. From mountain summits, we could see the spreading loss of wild lands and forests. We saw the air quality deteriorate as the distant mountains became less clear. With this background and experience many of us were drawn to organizations whose aim was caring for nature and preserving wild lands.

By the 1960s we felt an urgent need to preserve unprotected wild areas that we knew and treasured. We focused on what we knew and loved. We did not always connect our concern for these special areas with a more general approach to caring for nature. Our efforts tended to be piecemeal, focusing on conservation of forest land and preservation of *unique wild areas*. We were also concerned about water and air pollution and toxic chemicals in our food. There were differences between those who followed John Muir and the preservation movement, and those who supported conservation for wise resource use. Muir expressed a love for the inherent value of wild beings and places, whereas Gifford Pinchot and others emphasized stewardship and wise resource use as necessary for human well being. We did not originally see how all of these concerns could be served by means of a *wider unified environmental movement.*

Many of us were politically active in conservation organizations which worked for more parks and wilderness areas and to encourage wise resource use and conservation. By the end of the 1960s we realized that our efforts could fail if focused only on special areas. Preserved lands, we saw, are affected by their larger regions; the problems, we realized, are often international in scope. We sought a more unified approach that brought all our concerns together. We shifted our perspectives in fundamental ways. We were inspired by

Rachel Carson's book *Silent Spring* (1962), which ushered in a major change in our understanding of environmental issues. We began to see *how* they are interrelated. Carson helped us to see how our separate activities and their impacts are *interconnected in the natural world*. She helped us to see the natural world from the perspective of a field ecologist. She helped us to realize that the problems are often not just local, but can be systemic and even global. They are interconnected with our cultural values and technology practices. We better understood the interrelated nature of food web processes in the natural world, and how human systems interact with these ecosystems. During the 1960s global systems studies also underscored basic messages in Carson's book.

Carson helped us to realize something we tacitly knew from our own observations. When we view a whole watershed in a natural park, we know that the movement of water is an interrelated and interconnected process. From the ridge tops and high snow fields, to rivulets, streams, and rivers in valleys, to the distant marine estuaries, is an interconnected process. What we put into the watershed, from the summit to the valley below, is part of the whole system. The rain that falls on the mountain tops ends up in the sea. The atmosphere is also a dynamic interrelated process connecting the landscapes and seas, as it brings the rain storms in from the ocean. Carson describes the natural world as an interrelated process of living beings and energy flows forming complex and complementary relationships; the local niches and communities are all within larger ecosystem wholes. We are part of these processes within these ecosystem fields and energy flows. We participate in these systems. We decide how we will act in these relationships. We cannot choose to live outside of them. We affect them and they affect us. We became aware of our ecological effects and responsibilities.

During the 1960s the grass roots movements for social justice and peace helped to spur the movement for responsible treatment of the natural world. The dawning awareness that we are damaging ecosystems and habitats led to the national and international environmental movement. By the early 1970s people active in environmental research and policy studies realized that we need a comprehensive and global approach to these problems. We need actions at the local, regional, and international levels. A series of publications outlined the effects of human industrial activity on the natural environment. One influential series of studies was sponsored by the Club of Rome. Their first book in 1972 by D. H. and D. L. Meadows was entitled *The Limits to Growth*. Despite shortcomings, these studies underscored the *systemic and interrelated nature of the problems*, and how human activities impact the built and natural world. These studies united ecology with systems research. Systems studies had already made major contributions to research and development in industry. They enabled us to get a view of how whole systems work down to local details. The development of the air transport system, for example, would not have been possible without these whole systems, these interdisciplinary approaches. Teams of researchers included such disciplines as literature, anthropology, physics, and engineering. Two recent systems studies in the tradition of *Limits to Growth* are the *Ecological Footprint* (1992) by Bill Rees and Mathias Wackernagal, and *The Chaos Point: The World at the Crossroads* (2006) by Ervin Laszlo.

In the universities and colleges we studied environmental problems to learn how education and research can improve our relations with the natural world. We realized that our specialized approaches to knowledge were too limited. We needed to see the *natural world as a whole with us in it*. Our discussions were difficult at times because of the specialized languages of our different subjects and fields. The world, we realized, is not divided into subjects and disciplines. Specialized experts can miss the larger implications of what our technologies are doing. Academic disciplines are cultural creations that have advantages for detailed specialized knowledge with short term purposes. The interconnected processes of the natural world have much longer time spans and larger interconnected areas. The challenge is to effectively address environmental problems and issues in *comprehensive and deep ways*.

Public concern grew more widespread as the seriousness of environmental problems became generally recognized. Governments created environmental protection agencies, laws and policies that required mitigating actions. Colleges and universities created programs in environmental education and research. We debated whether to have awareness raising programs, or more comprehensive approaches to redesign our economic and technology systems. The first Earth Day, started by U.S. Senator Gaylord Nelson, was held on

April 22, 1970. In 1971 Earth Day was officially endorsed by U Thant and the United Nations. Celebrations were held around the world and on campuses all over North America. A host of new institutes, schools, programs, departments, and committees were created. There were new journals, other publications, areas of research and learning programs. Some of these efforts were experimental as we sought to learn *how to create effective cross cultural, interdisciplinary environmental research and education.*

ES at the University of Victoria (UVic)

At UVic Marc Bell, Derrick Sewell and other faculty members brought forth proposals to address environmental issues on our campus. They recommended an approach to Environmental Studies (ES) that could be implemented with low cost in a short time. A comprehensive proposal surfaced in 1972 which was circulated to the Arts and Sciences faculty for comment. In 1974 Arts and Sciences Dean Jean-Paul Vinay established a committee to implement key elements in the proposal. This was the beginning of the University wide experimental program in Environmental Studies. This program was approved by the faculty of Arts and Sciences with the condition that it be reviewed in four years. In 1978 the program had an extensive review. The steering committee submitted their report with a number of recommendations. The main proposal was that ES be made a regular interdisciplinary program with its own director and steering committee. These recommendations were approved by the faculty of Arts and Sciences, the University Senate, and the Board of Governors. Thus in 1979 ES became a regular campus program that evolved into the School of Environmental Studies by 1999. Many students and faculty were involved in the early phases of ES development on our campus. After 36 years most of the aims of the program pioneers have been realized.

In the early years we had many discussions about how best to develop an ES program to address the issues raised by serious environmental problems. The most comprehensive proposal was for a broadly based interdisciplinary institute devoted to research and education in environmental problems and issues. Such an undertaking requires substantial resources in funds, personnel, and space. Some universities undertook such ambitious programs, but at UVic we started in a gradual way. As an experimental program with almost no budget, we borrowed our personnel, courses, space, and resources from existing departments. The first committee to oversee the program had seven to eight members who were from the Humanities, Social Sciences, and the Life and Physical Sciences. Members of the original committee were Peter Murphy (from Geography, the first Chair), George Beer, Martin Hocking, Marc Bell, Alan Drengson, and Rennie Warburton. Also on the committee in the early years were Herb Smith, Steve Webb, Gerald Walters, and Alan Austin.

During the early years some thought that environmental problems could be solved mostly by technical means through science and technology. We can modify our systems, but not change our basic values and attitudes toward the Earth. Others, in the social sciences, for example in economics and political science, thought that economic and policy matters should be the main focus. Some in the humanities thought these problems involve our ultimate values and personal philosophies in conflict with the values of the ecosphere. Clearly, all aspects of the problems needed to be addressed. It was difficult then to say which should have priority. Since our program used existing resources, it had a number of different focuses and themes, depending on the interests and fields of study of those involved including students. We went through the university calendar with colleagues from various disciplines to identify relevant courses. We encouraged creating new courses to address issues in specific fields. Over time new courses were introduced such as environmental psychology by Robert Gibson, environmental economics by Leonard Ladidao, environmental philosophy by Alan Drengson, a natural resource course by Bill Ross, and an ecology course tailored to the Environmental Studies program.

We learned with experience what worked, and also what could be removed from program descriptions. The first Environmental Studies course, ES 300, was added in 1975. This interdisciplinary course was designed to bring ES students and faculty together for discussions and shared projects. Marc Bell led this course in its early years. It was problem oriented, emphasized group process, and provided off campus and interdisciplinary experience. ES 300 had many memorable events such as design-ins with Stan King and weekends at Yellow Point Lodge near Ladysmith. This was the first of many ES courses. There also were double listed ES Courses mentioned above such as ES 314 also was listed as Philosophy 333.

The chair of the ES steering committee was rotated between the members from different departments and faculties. The ES Program was eventually under the Dean of Social Sciences when the Arts and Sciences Faculty split into three divisions. During the review in 1978 the chair of the committee, Alan Drengson, taught one course less than normal load in order to conduct the review and administer the program. He served a number of terms on the Steering Committee. From 1979 on there was continuing development of courses and research into expanding areas of interest such as environmental law and politics. Today in the university community, and on other campuses, are publications on environmental literature, ecoliterature, ecocriticism, environmental history, and so on. There are courses to train teachers in environmental education within the Education Faculty. There is work relevant to Environmental Studies in art, music, and history of art. A major area added to the UVic ES Program is Ecological Restoration first headed by Don Eastman in 1999. Don developed a number of courses in restoration and students also did studies on restoration efforts in various places off campus.

Since its inception the ES Program at UVic has provided a lot of synergy within the University and with the larger community. Looking back, many of our advanced research programs reflect the *methods and purposes we used to integrate our separate disciplines* to meet the challenges of the environmental crisis. We learned how to communicate complexity in more open and simple ways. We learned to communicate across disciplines and how to cooperate and pool our resources for effective action and learning. There was a tremendous growth in library and other media resources. By 1989 the ES Program had become a Department with Full Time Equivalents (FTEs), tenured professors, and a regular budget within the Faculty of Social Sciences. Duncan Taylor was the first FTE and was appointed in 1986 as a Sessional and then in 1989 as an Assistant Professor. He introduced a number of ES Courses, such as ES300A/B Environmental Perspectives and Environmental Issues, which was completely redesigned from the 300 version Marc Bell had taught. Over the years, Taylor also introduced ES 414 Introduction to Natural and Social Systems, ES 400A/B Advanced Systems Theory, ES 404 Discourses of Environmentalism, ES 412 Canada in Transition, and ES 380 Introduction to Integral Systems Theory and Practice.

During the next phase of development we created the first joint Chair of Environmental Studies with the Faculty of Law, currently held by Michael M'Gonigle who came in 1995. We had a full term Director, Paul West, secretarial and marking assistants, and students on every level, including grad studies. Students can do a double major in ES and another discipline. They can also do a minor in ES. They can do Special Arrangement Graduate Degrees which are chaired by interdisciplinary committees. In 2000 the program had 15 graduate students. Paul West served one of the longest terms as Director from 1987 to 2001, and he also received an environmental research grant in Chemistry. Under Paul's direction the program developed in several dimensions and eventually became a School. He also introduced the ES Course in Environmental Protection (originally ES 432).

Some of the other faculty, who served as Chair before ES became a School in 1999 were Bill Ross, Marc Bell, and Gerry Walter. Some of the committee members during the next phase were Eric Roth, Rob Walker, Bill Carroll, Steve Lonegran, Phil Dearden, Geraldine Allen, Michele Pujol, Malcolm Rutherford, Mike Edgell, Gloria Snively, Chris Tollefson, Rod Dobell, Richard Ring, and Victoria Wyatt. Sharon Nicolson was the longtime administrative assistant to the program and her contribution to its operation was invaluable. There were also many Sessional Instructors invaluable to the program such as Angus Taylor, Thomas Heyd, Sarah Hutchinson, Doug Patterson, Bob Hay, Paul Senez, Jamie Allan, Susan Abs, and Fiona Chambers. There were also other faculty members Wendy Wickwire who came in 1995, Karena Shaw, John Volpe and Val Shaefer also are part of the ES School. Richard Hebda made valuable contributions to the Restoration Program. Eric Higgs became the Director in 2002.

There is now an extensive program in Ecological Restoration. The ES Law Chair held by Michael M'Gonigle has its own research budget and assistants. Our undergraduate program is one of the oldest in

Canada and North America. We have graduated many students, who have earned advanced degrees in other Canadian Universities and elsewhere. We attract students from all over Canada and the world. Many distinctions have been bestowed on our faculty and students. We have a tradition with a high level of energy focused on our shared concern for the natural world and human well being. Our students have contributed many leading edge projects to our school such as solar water heating, and they play a role in campus sustainability and other initiatives. Our school contributes to local and provincial communities, and also has an international presence. We successfully recommended persons for Lansdowne Fellowships such as Arne Naess in 1988 and visiting scholars and honorary degrees such as Merve Wilkinson in 2005. Faculty members like Nancy Turner, who came in 1990, have won many national and international honors. Turner was our first tenured full professor. She introduced many new courses such as ES 321 Ethnoecology, ES421 Enthnobotany: Plants and Human Cultures, and ES 423 Traditional Systems of Land and Resource Management. She has done extensive research with first nations' cultures in British Columbia. In 2010 she was awarded the Order of Canada for her work. She earlier received the Order of British Columbia in 1999 for her distinguished scholarship and work with British Columbia's aboriginal people.

When we started Environmental Studies in 1974, we had a budget of $2500 with no space or FTEs of our own. We can look back with great satisfaction at the distance we have traveled as an academic community devoted to deep and sustainable values that benefit humans and our companion beings on planet Earth. There have been many exciting and important events, lectures, and conferences we have sponsored, that have not been mentioned here, as well as other courses developed, such as those related to sustainability and restoration.

There is now a resurgence of public support for environmental actions similar to the early 1970s. There is action in government and society to address the complex problems and issues like global warming and loss of biological and cultural diversity. Through the years we realized in ES that we were helping to bring about a major transition in our society and personal lives. We realized in the 1970s that we could not go on with business as usual. The Earth's ecosystems have limits. Our population effects are magnified by industrial technologies and massive fossil fuel use not designed for or compatible with long term sustainability. We need to change our policies and practices to live more wisely and to avoid major degradation of our life support systems. The ultimate aim of higher learning is a life time commitment to creative inquiry and high *quality of life*. The environmental crisis calls on us to respect the complex values of our ecological communities and honor our responsibilities to each other and other beings. We can shift our focus to quality of life issues, while we lower our impacts on the environment. With wise design of lifestyles and practices, we can have a high *quality of life* and a much lower impact on the world. How we treat the natural world is a shared concern related to peace and social justice. Caring for our home place and the Earth is an obligation that transcends our generation, cultures, nations, and special interests.

In the early years of the environmental movement there was a wide consensus on how to proceed. The activists then (as now) came from all areas on the political and cultural spectrums. *Environmental quality should not be a partisan matter.* We recognize the critical importance of our shared home, and the inestimable value of its treasured places as common goods to be cared for responsibly by *all of us*. We recognize that although people have different personal philosophies, worldviews, religions and political views, *we can cooperate for the common good* of our shared Earth. The environment is not a special interest but our common home. Nations recognize that cooperation to protect the natural world is necessary across all national, cultural and religious boundaries. We should be in a race for excellent care of the Earth and all beings. Movements are always changing and adapting to the conditions of our world. Laws and policies need to evolve, as well as our actions in our home places. The front of the environmental movement is long and deep. There is something we each can do to improve quality of life, our relations with each other and with the Earth. Our Lansdowne Lecturer Arne Naess suggested we can do this if we each act *beautifully* by giving back more than we receive from our Earth Household Places.

ALAN DRENGSON is Professor Emeritus of Philosophy and Adjunct Professor of Environmental and Graduate Studies at the University of Victoria in Canada. His areas are Eastern philosophy, comparative religion, environmental philosophy, and multicultural technology studies. He teaches and practices meditation disciplines aiming for harmony with Nature, such as Aikido. He loves wild dancing, skiing, wilderness journeying, and mountaineering. He has published many articles and books (for example, *The Practice of Technology, Beyond Environmental Crisis* and *Wild Way Home*) and recently finished two book manuscripts *Caring for Home Place* and *Being at Home with One's Self.* He is the author of *Doc Forest and Blue Mountain Ecostery*, an ecotopian novel, and of three poetry books the *Sacred Journey Series.* He is Associate Editor for the 10 Volume *Selected Works of Arne Naess* published by Springer in 2005. He is coeditor of five anthologies: *The Philosophy of Society; The Deep Ecology Movement; Ecoforestry: The Art and Science of Sustainable Forest Use; Ecology of Wisdom: Writings by Arne Naess;* and *Wild Foresting: Practicing Nature's Wisdom.* He is founding editor of the online journal *The Trumpeter: Journal of Ecosophy* and of the journal *Ecoforestry.* He does workshops in the *Wild Way,* and presented in the Massey Symposium at the University of Toronto's Massey College in March 2005. In spring 2008 he was Visiting Professor in Canadian Studies at Simon Fraser University in Burnaby BC and taught "Multiculturalism, Sense of Place and Personal Identity". Contact: alandren@uvic.ca. For samples of his work see www.ecostery.org and http://trumpeter.athabascau.ca.

"Buck in Grasses" copyright © 2011 by Chris Westlund. Photo taken in Washington State, USA.

"Attachment" copyright © 2011 by Anne Westlund. Photo taken at the Grays Harbor County Fair, Washington State, USA.

A Natural Setting

Anne Westlund

Westlund, A. (2011). A natural setting. *Restoration Earth: An Interdisciplinary Journal for the Study of Nature & Civilization*, *1*(1), 34. Copyright © The Authors. All rights reserved. For reprint information contact: oceanseminary@verizon.net.

Seeing your plants in a new light
no light, full moon obscured.

Do you wonder what I'm doing?
Up so early, before the big show.
Before the opening curtain,
daylight just minutes away.

Or do you know?
Hands trailing
in the potted plants. Fingers
exploring the offerings from
the soil.

It's not that we're blind,
it's that we don't care enough.
To you, every feather is numbered
on every bird, every hair on every head,
all the leaves on all the plants.

Hands wet with dew and rain,
it pleases me greatly,
that You have touched all this,
before me, before any of us.

ANNE WESTLUND's poem "Fur" was published in the Marshall Creek Project Fall Newsletter in 2009. She is putting together a book of poetry based on the Viking Runes. *Lifelines*, a book of poetry by the Poetic Muselings, an online poetry critique group that Anne has been involved in since its inception, has been picked up for publication this fall. Anne is enrolled in a Masters program for Interfaith Studies. When not studying she can be found crafting, cooking, playing computer mahjong or surfing creativity websites. She lives in Western Washington, near the coast with her family and cat, Betty Boop. She loves to take photographs of nature's beauty and share them with others. Contact: sasquatch2008@gmail.com

Homework

Florence R. Shepard

Shepard, F. R. (2011). Homework. *Restoration Earth: An Interdisciplinary Journal for the Study of Nature & Civilization, 1*(1), 35–41.

Home. Like a mantra, the word resonates within us. At best, it conjures up childhood grounding in the context of family and place. At worst, as with children orphaned in devastated landscapes of war or natural disaster, it may recall a nightmare of deprivation. But whether colored with nostalgia and sentimentality or ambivalence and regret, the word is loaded with symbolism.

My thoughts often return to homes that have sheltered me. Interestingly my experiences with these dwellings over my long life closely recapitulate the history of modern homemaking in western culture. My hope, in sharing some of these thoughts, is that they contain elements that are trans- cultural and common to all people of all ages who share this Earth home and try to create within it a suitable lived-in space.

When I speak of home, I am not merely referring to a house. A house is a structure that can be perceived objectively from many angles: square feet, showcase, investment, inheritance, status symbol, artistic statement, shelter, sanctuary, technological wonder, cell or nest, modern wonder or relic of the past. Whereas building a house is a task that can be accomplished in a set period of time, making a home is a lifetime undertaking and, rather than being a discrete structure, it is a complex amalgam of personal values, culture and geography.

Homes are easier to imagine than to make. In writing, I can choose happy romantic images and ignore the ambiguous or troubling ones tucked out of sight like old clothes in a trunk. I can paint an immaculate scene, a spotless house awaiting company, without washing on the line or dirty dishes in the sink. Unlike the sanitized perfections pictured in journals, making a home is messier and demands much attention and hard work from its inhabitants.

Householding is the term usually associated with owning a home. A legal deed, however, is not a prerequisite for homemaking. Some of our first dwellings—boarding houses, college dormitories, rented rooms or apartments—are staging grounds from which we leave home and commence our life journey. These first attempts, that may include "playing house" in childhood, involve searching for, as well as imagining, a future home. Although occupied as temporary holding places, such dwellings infused with personal investment, can become permanent domiciles.

The search for home for men and women, as Alan Block insightfully postulates, may be more about leaving or finding a home one can return to rather than making one (Block, 2010). Some pure souls, who take the quest for home seriously, may set out to find an acceptable environment and then literally build their home from the ground up. The home then becomes an explicit example of their lived values.

However it may be construed, making a home requires time and sensitivity to place, forethought and sustained commitment. Yet a simple shelter from the elements as well as a permanent structure can fill the basic requirements of an ideal home, a place where comfort, safety, and well-being are assured and beauty can enter (Rybczynski, 1987).

Before the late nineteenth century, houses in Western cultures grew to palatial dimensions as symbols of wealth and power. The poor, if lucky enough to have a shelter of any sort, were crowded into one-room hovels void of comfort and privacy. Houses grew proportionately as wealth accumulated and, in some cases, required hundreds of domestic servants to provide minimal comforts for owners. All houses, from great halls and castles to ordinary homes, were without plumbing, inefficiently heated, poorly ventilated and minimally lighted. Many servants were needed by the wealthy to keep fires burning in fireplaces, carry water for bathing and personal hygiene, tote away wastes and prepare meals (Bryson, 2010).

Along with the growth of the middle class in the United States during the nineteenth century, there was a social movement toward better health. Cleanliness and efficiency were embedded in this new ethic. Most of the technological wonders of modern homes were invented and adapted for households during the thirty years from 1890 to 1920. The first electrical appliances did not reduce the tedium of housework, however, since they were cumbersome and difficult to manipulate. If other jobs were available, women workers preferred almost anything, including factory work, to "domestic service" (Rybczynkski, 1986, p. 159).

Bill Bryson (2010) makes the interesting observation that the first electrical conveniences touted for reducing the work of homemakers were designed to eliminate work previously done by men, such as chopping wood, and were actually of little benefit to women. Prosperity reigned at the turn of the century and houses grew bigger but so did expectations for more complicated meals and cleanliness. Concomitantly, women's work in the home increased.

Although making a home should not be misconstrued as simply housekeeping, in my experience as with many working class women, the two are closely aligned. That is not to say that making a home for many women and men in our modern society is not pleasurable and, in some cases, a chosen life work. Although challenging, it can be a creative and satisfying enterprise. Similar to important relationships with humans, it requires a tremendous investment of spiritual and material resources, as well as personal time and energy. With homes, however, the effort is expended toward something that is material and inanimate.

Eugene Halton (1981), in his fascinating study of households, interviewed families concerning the objects they collected and displayed in their homes. He found that collected and valued objects did not hold the same meaning for the various members of a family. Nonetheless, some objects, which embodied the values of the inhabitants, frequently became integrating forces in the lives of family members.

Collected objects, as well as pets, however, can become all-consuming elements in a home. To the extent that the residents cannot imagine their lives without them, these objects may take on a life of their own. Failing to detach from such perceived treasures, ailing elders in need of care, may allow death, the ultimate arbiter, to make that final separation for them.

Fond or painful formative images of childhood homes are forever etched on our minds. Out of deep memory come poignant images of my first dwelling, an old log house built along a river on a sheep ranch in southwestern Wyoming. Nature was at its door, and the entire surround, of farm buildings and river and meadows and willows, was home to us as well. From these memories I conclude that both the house and the natural environment, in which it is situated, are important to the developing child.

Each season offered a plethora of adventures. In summers of early childhood, I spent hours in summer exploring an oxbow pond nearby that teemed with water creatures: frogs and tadpoles and ephemeral blue dragonflies dancing on its surface. This "flow time," when I was immersed in the experience of the moment, bonded me to nature forevermore (Csikszentimihalyi, 1975; cited in Csikszentimaihalyi & Halton, 1981, p. 185).

With my two sisters, I searched daily through a compound of interconnecting ranch buildings near the log house for eggs laid surreptitiously in well-hidden nests by free-ranging chickens. On these adventurous forays we followed a course in and out and through the structures that morphed into games of hide-and-go-seek. I recall the excitement and unfettered delight of running pell-mell through this labyrinthine course with one or the other sibling in pursuit, immersed in spontaneous, deep play, an essential ingredient of childhood.

The spirit of exploration, needed by children led us further afield to nearby maze-like sheep trails through densely growing willows. With our mother's permission, we sometimes ran to a nearby ridge where under a rocky shelter in fire pits left by archaic nomadic tribes, we searched for shiny flint chards, treasures from the past.

In winter, after playing in and exploring deep drifts of snow in the yard, we returned to the warmth of the log house, familiar territory where I wandered to my heart's content: examining each room, looking out each window and into each space, studying designs in the old sagging wallpaper and cracked paint, taking in the aroma of pantries and closets. When I tired of exploring the house as it was, I turned it upside down with a self-designed game as I walked through the house staring with total concentration into my mother's hand mirror held at chin level and parallel to the ceiling. This simulated fly's view created the exciting illusion of walking on the ceiling and stepping over doorsills and around light fixtures.

In the evenings, after a busy day of exploration, I crawled into a tiny space behind the coal-fired kitchen stove. With the hot water tank at my back and the warm linoleum under my body, I would fall asleep, lulled by the conversations between my father and compatriot ranch hands, sitting around the oilcloth-covered table, sharing in Italian their "old country" tales. Mamma would eventually extricate me from my "hidey hole" and carry me to bed.

As the winter broke and the snow melted, the natural world came alive once more. At daybreak and in evening light, I stood on tiptoes at the open upstairs bedroom window mesmerized by the pulsing cadence of breeding frogs. In those days of early childhood, I was filled with a sense of wonder and anticipation, as if gestating, awaiting the revelations of a fully lived life. The topography of my early childhood home, the house and natural surround, were rich and filled with wonder—but always within reach of my mother's voice and gentle hand. The hallmark of domesticity, she was the center of my universe.

My mother was born to an immigrant Italian family and my father came to America from Austrian Tyrol as a teenager. My parents exerted great effort to raise us as "Americans." When, as an adult, I visited their homeland, I discovered they had failed in this effort. On that riverbank in Wyoming they had reconstituted a little Italy.

At about the time I lost my "baby" teeth, biology and family norms forced me to "grow up" and become an integral part of the working ranch and household. When my parents moved to the ranch in the late twenties, modern technology was available in cities but rural electrification was unavailable. My mother moved from a home that was furbished with electric stove and iron, refrigerator and dish and clothes washers to a ranch home with coal stoves for heating, kerosene lanterns, an icebox, a hand pump in the kitchen for water and an outhouse. My father quickly installed an "electric plant", a diesel generator, to provide electricity and we soon had running water and an indoor bathroom. In order to conserve electricity for pumping water, however, we often ironed clothes with stove irons and used kerosene or gas lanterns for light.

These were days of the Great Depression and of mass foreclosures, when my deeply indebted parents struggled for survival and subsisted through the efforts of the entire family to save our ranch home. On through the days of World War II when the able men had gone to war, we three daughters in the summer took on both men's work and women's work, which included housekeeping, gardening, milking and tending domestic animals and putting up the hay for winter fodder. With daily chores completed, we spent leisure time, when it existed, swimming, riding horseback, reading, or embroidering. After entering college through the war years, I returned each summer to help with the ranch work. In that ranch home during those early years, the seeds of love, frugality, sustainability, hard work and family unity were sown that form the foundation of my life.

Sun streamed through south-facing windows onto polished wooden floors. Hand-sown window dressings matched brightly painted walls. The echo of laughter and activity of children threaded through gatherings of family and friends. This was the home where my first husband and I raised our children. When we married, we bought the house from a miner who had built it from old company houses salvaged from an abandoned coal camp. Although somewhat unimaginative, it was built to last, with a good foundation and structure and solid wood floors and woodwork. The stucco on the exterior was imbedded with pieces of colored glass the likes of which I have seen only in Scotland, the builder's homeland.

In this house in that post–World War II era I stepped into the role of women socialized to domesticity and housekeeping skills. Cleanliness, efficiency and proper nutrition were promulgated through "homemaking clubs." Because of the smoke created by the coal-fired furnaces, "spring cleaning," scrubbing walls and floors and every nook and cranny in the house, was a socially instituted and accepted housekeeping ritual. Like most middle class women, I was a "stay at home mom" where I was expected to care for our children and the household.

Similarly to many domestics and housewives, I found housework tedious and read books such as *I Hate to Housekeep,* aimed at simplifying the process (Bracken, 1977). Through the years, I honed the art of simple and easy living, limiting household appurtenances and developing habits of conservation of energy and frugality that limited consumption. Cooking became an escape from the toil and suppression of housework and allowed for some creativity and experimentation. The cookbook I followed was literally worn to shambles as if it had been taken up in a tornado.

Likewise, I followed the norm of conventional child rearing practices according to Dr. Benjamin Spock (1945) who proposed permissive but attentive methods. My four children—a scientist, a builder, an explorer, and an inventor—grew up with freedom to express their creativity and talents and to roam freely and safely in nature in a nearby gulley or in the small community at large. They extended their territories in summer to the forested mountains where we camped, hiked and fished and in winter with skating and sledding with friends and skiing with me.

When serious health problems incapacitated my husband, I put my college degree in zoology to work and became a biology teacher. Teaching, a profession I had never considered, surprisingly became a passion and constant and beguiling challenge. It disrupted the protective insulation and isolation of housekeeping and led me to a self-fulfilling life, drawing me out of my home but not out of domesticity and "shadow work" (Illich, 1981). Like many working mothers, I tried to carry on with the household per usual and meet the demands of career. At times when I hired domestic help, I felt guilty for doing so.

Like a protective cover shielding a fragile antique couch from harm, my efforts to make a secure and attractive home, according to the mandates of society, church and extended family, masked the oppression I felt in my marriage. After two decades of being the proper wife, in mid-life I faced my failed marriage and left husband, home and community, with three teenage children (by then my older daughter had married) to pursue a doctorate and begin a university teaching career.

It was then that I purchased an old house on "The Avenues", an older section of the city where I was close to work, neighbors and downtown and removed from the sprawl of suburbia. I paid a pittance for the house—red brick, two-story, prairie style, a century old—that was built to last. From the first moment I saw it, I knew it would make a good home. It became the best material investment of my lifetime and a sanctuary for my children and me.

Although in close proximity to other houses, it had a large unkempt backyard with a huge English walnut tree. Through the years I developed a flower and vegetable garden and planted fruit trees, berry bushes, and grape vines. The natural world seeped in and drew me out as a witness to the progression of seasons: traces of green tulip and daffodil spikes, bird song, buds and seedlings, pink lady butterflies, nesting birds, flowers and fruit, the turning of leaves…. Birds dropped by in proper time leaving me wide-eyed at the biological necessity that drew them back each year. Following the harvest and preservation of vegetables and fruit, the garden eased into the stony silence of winter. Circumpolar navigating waxwings feasted on pyracantha berries, leaving little red, polka-dotted scat on the sidewalks. From the vantage point of my backyard, I confronted the universe, from ripe raspberry to comet.

Unbeknownst to me at the time of purchase of the house, what I thought was a dead-end at the end of the block was, in fact, a stairway to City Creek Canyon, an urban park with trails that extend up the canyon along a sparkling creek and into the high mountains. Daily walks in this natural area became a source of healing and refuge for me. As the ranch house had, this house became a doorway to nature.

I had no funds for properly refurbishing the old house but that did not diminish the pleasure of living in it. Even with a somewhat shabby interior, it had a welcoming ambience. Much of my homework and that of my children took place at an old dining-room table brought from my childhood ranch home. Sitting there in the subdued light at dusk I would ease into a meditative mood tracing the contours of the house and my life.

From the butler's pantry and beyond into the kitchen, my eyes followed the lines to the entrance hall, the living room, and up the stairs. Angles of ceiling and moldings, doorways and trim, cabinets and windows, fit into each other in harmonious progression. The structure itself invited contemplation as well as habitation. Back door to front door, upstairs and down, primal refuge and intimate space, cradle and camp, this home was a place from which I calculated my course and started a new life.

The home was also a doorway to community. From any window or door, I could see neighbors' homes, if not the neighbors themselves. In the evening from my bedroom I viewed the city stretching out across the valley. In the morning, as carillons sounded from churches and the state capitol, I stood at the upstairs hall window surveying the backyards, a maze of fences, garages, electric wires, and driveways, which, at the turn of the century, were courtyards for carriages. I fantasized about bringing cohesion to the block by tearing down the fences, building underground parking or shedding our cars, and creating a communal garden and a safe play area for small children and arbors where elders could visit. This plan, which demanded radical social change, remained a dream. Seduced by the idea of property and privacy, we cordoned off our yards from each other. Yet there was much neighborly reciprocity, especially with proximate neighbors.

After several false starts and returns home, my children grew up and left home to commence lives of their own. It was then I met and married Paul Shepard, a scholar of human ecology. He settled comfortably into the Avenue's home, similar to the one of his childhood on a hilltop in Missouri, from which as a child he went forth each day to explore the surrounding woods. Frequent research forays took us abroad to all parts of the globe. On a July day, a little more than a decade after we met, Paul died in this home one summer day as the sound of crickets entered the open windows and drew him back to his place of origin.

Paul and I lived an entire lifetime during the decade we shared. As we traveled, I was able to observe something that since childhood had been my preoccupation: the domestic activities of women, busy in their "vernacular" work whose toils reflected my mother's work and my own (Illich, 1982). It touched my heart to see women involved in "shadow work," the kind of grinding, unpaid toil, which goes unnoticed world-wide yet sustains household and national economies (Illich, 1981).

India, in particular, offered innumerable variations on the householding theme, many along the roadside and in clear view. We stayed at the Indian Institute of Science in Bangalore for several months and ventured out periodically to various sites as Paul conducted research for a book on the relationships between animals and people (Shepard, 1998).

One memorable evening Paul and I hired a man on his bicycle rickshaw to drive us to the outskirts of a city. The din of traffic on crowded streets had ebbed. Beyond a bridge that crossed a river, vender's stalls, open to view, lined the road. All was still except for a low murmur, like the buzzing of bees, which puzzled me until I recognized it as the sound of people conversing quietly over their evening meal. In the stalls, families gathered around stacked cooking pots, sharing food and thoughts of the day. Whether they lived in the structures or went to another home following their meal, I did not know. But the unforgettable mumur of their voices, which I still recall vividly, told me they were very much at home.

We visited the house, which Mahatma Gandhi had built as a model of elegant simplicity and ecological sensitivity. I remember it, clean, white, airy, filled with light from high windows that also provided cross ventilation. It was a small home, with a sitting room, bedroom and two tiny cubicles at the rear: in one, an efficient kitchen; in the other, a bathroom that demonstrated how to maintain personal cleanliness and dispose of human wastes organically. The structure itself and the plastered walls provided its interior décor. Furnishings and personal effects were held to a minimum. Gandhi had many options for how to live. He built this very simple and efficient home, which became a microcosm of cultural transformation, as an example for others.

Back in the United States, Paul and I purchased a few acres of meadowland in the Hoback Basin in Wyoming and built a small cabin. The land was part of an old homestead fed by a ditch that followed the archaic course of an intermittent stream. He was an avid fisherman and the surrounding streams offered a plethora of trout; I was thrilled to return to Wyoming, the place of my birth. Willows enclosed the meadowland, which bordered designated United States National Forest where the sagebrush steppe habitat sloped up into an aspen and spruce–fir forest on the ramparts of mountains that encircled the Basin.

Before exploration and settlement of this land, the Shoshone indigenous tribes traveled through this region, following migratory routes of animals that were their major source of food. Each campsite was

39

home to them, familiar territory with water and protection. Material objects and personal possessions were held to a minimum to lighten loads on their journeys. In the fall, with provisions of dried meat and berries, they began their return to their lowland wintering grounds in Utah and Idaho. Seasonal migrations were in synchrony with the cycles of Planet Earth that they recognized as their true home and mother.

As we planned the building of our cabin, Paul and I walked on the land in daytime to consider orientation to the sun and, after dark, the position of the stars. Throughout the planning the image of Mahatma Gandhi's model home was always on our minds. The final product was a small, energy efficient cabin with windows on all sides: on the south for solar heat and on the north to frame the Gros Ventre Mountains in daytime and Ursa Major and Minor at night. I have returned to the cabin in Wyoming each spring for twenty years, the last fifteen after Paul's death. My yearly journeys to and from my Utah home follow the approximate migratory route of past indigenous people on their annual journeys.

What is most intriguing about the cabin is the wonder of nature's diversity at my door. In spring, which comes late in this high steppe country, dawn or dusk choruses of nesting birds ignite the soul. Their songs serve a proprietary function and establish integrated blending of individual bird territories that form a bio-diverse habitat within the Greater Yellowstone Bioregion. At the close and opening of each day the symphony is complemented by the songs of breeding frogs, the yipping of coyotes, and an occasional howl of a wolf. By midsummer, adult birds fly surreptitiously back and forth feeding hungry hatchlings. Feisty little hummingbirds go to battle for nectar in my garden flowers and feed at my feeders, often confronting me eye to eye.

From my cabin cage, I observe mammals of all stripes pass by my windows or settle in my yard. Myriads of mice and voles make tender pickings for the hawks that cruise the meadow or use my rooftop as a staging site for hunts. Small prairie mammals—pocket gophers, ground squirrels, skunks, weasels, badgers, foxes, and coyotes—den near or hunt in my yard, feasting on each other or pickings from my compost.

Large herbivores of this high mountain basin pass by the cabin or use my few acres for grazing. A wary pronghorn doe may find a suitable place on the sagebrush knoll to birth her fawn and bed it for the day near the cabin where she has learned it will be safe. Under her constant vigil, it will sprout to almost adult size in a few short months. Deer spend their days out of sight in the dense willows along the river and pass by at dusk on their way to the forest on the butte where they feed at night to return at dawn to their willow arbor for protection. A lone cow moose and her calf often wander through at night and bed down in the willows leaving their scat as calling cards. By the time I return to my cabin each year, elk have migrated from their winterfeeding grounds about a mile away, and have returned to the high meadows where they birth and raise their young near alpine meadows where tender new grasses are plentiful.

Many animals make their homes permanently in this region, and have evolved over-wintering adaptations, from dormant larval forms to hibernation or winter sleep. In winter the larger ungulates migrate to warmer climates to the south; some birds fly to the far reaches of the southern hemisphere. But whatever the pattern, the life cycle of each animal is wired for survival: finding shelter, breeding and raising young, avoiding predators, but, most importantly, maintaining their strength by eating vegetation and, often, each other. Each finds a niche in their bio-diverse ecological home, kept healthy and balanced by top predators such as raptors and wolves. The animals offer a prayerful example of our own hallowed connection to them and to the Earth.

As I consider the artifacts of a lifetime of householding, I am drawn to a premise suggested by Thoreau, the ultimate housing authority: Life is rich in proportion to the number of things we can afford to let alone. For inspiration on homemaking I have turned repeatedly to Mahatma Gandhi, the master down-sizer, who, it is said, died with about ten personal possessions worth approximately two dollars.

Through a long and challenging lifetime, I have nurtured a primal ecological sensibility exalted by Paul Shepard (1973, 1998). A minimalist of sorts I have pared down material possessions and perfected the art easy housekeeping. Cherished objects, given and often made by family members, provide a "tangible sign" of the continuity of my life experiences, relationships and values (Halton, 1981). Having given over the old historical home to my daughter I now live nearby in a condominium. But I have never forfeited the role of mother, an unconditional and terminal condition, from which my offspring undoubtedly wish I'd be cured.

Through these peregrinations through the dwellings of my lifetime, I have come to appreciate the primary role homes have played in my wellbeing and the freedom, security, and privileges they have offered. Much more than assuring me creature comforts and privacy sequestered away from the cares of the world, my homes have been a doorway to community and nature. I have readily accepted the homework they entailed, knowing full well the necessity of this sustained relationship. For the most part, I now live alone in a very quiet and peaceful way, having found, amidst the many amenities of home, the comfort and solace of a solitary life. (Picard, 1964).

References

Block, A. A. (April, 2010). *Homecomings and leavings.* Unpublished paper presented at the annual meeting of the American Association for the Advancement of Curricular Studies, Denver, CO.

Bracken, P. (19770 I *hate to housekeep book.* New York: Harcourt, Brace and World.

Bryson, B. (2010). *At home, a short history of private life.* New York: Doubleday.

Csikszentmihalyi, M., & Rochberg-Halton, E. (1981). *The meanings of things, domestic symbols and the self.* United Kingdom: Cambridge University Press.

Halton, E. (2008). *The great brain suck.* Chicago: The University of Chicago Press.

Illich, I. (1981). *Shadow work.* Boston: Marion Boyers.

Illich, I. (1982). *Gender.* New York: Pantheon.

Martin, C. L. (2010). *The great forgetting.* Santa-Fe, CA: K-Selected Books.

Picard, M. (1964). *The world of silence.* Boston: Henry Regency Company.

Rybczynski, W. (1986). *Home, a short history of an idea.* New York: Penguin Books.

Shepard, P, (1996). *The others, how animals made us human.* Washington, DC: Island Press/Shearwater Books.

Shepard, P. (1998). *Coming home to the Pleistocene* (ed. Florence Shepard). Washington, DC: Island Press/Shearwater Books.

Shepard, P. (1998), *The tender carnivore and the sacred game.* Athens, GA: The University of George Press. (original publication 1973, New York: Charles Scribner's Sons).

Spock, B. (1945). *Baby and child care.* New York: Pocket Books.

✣✻✣

FLORENCE ROSE (KRALL) SHEPARD is Professor Emerita of Educational Studies, The University of Utah, where she taught educational, environmental, and feminist studies. She has published her personal narratives of place in journals, anthologies, and a book, *Ecotone* (SUNY Press, 1994) and edited and published Paul Shepard's posthumous books: *Coming Home to the Pleistocene* (Island Press, 1998), *Encounter With Nature* (Island Press, 1999), and *Where We Belong* (University of Georgia Press, 2003). Flo spends most of each year in a cabin in the Hoback Basin, Bondurant, Wyoming, and winters in Salt Lake City, Utah.

Commentary on Florence Shepard's "Homework"

Vidya Sarveswaran

Sarveswaran, V. (2011). Commentary on Florence Shepard's "homework". *Restoration Earth: An Interdisciplinary Journal for the Study of Nature & Civilization*, 1(1), 42. Copyright © The Authors. All rights reserved. For reprint information contact: oceanseminary@verizon.net.

This paper, which is a personal narrative by Dr. Florence Shepard, seeks to articulate the concept of "Home" and synthesizes her perceptions of home as an architectural, social, and cultural marker. Posited within a broad spectrum of plural meanings that home has to offer, Dr. Shepard's essay chronicles the consigning of her personal home from an historical habitat-dwelling to a condominium of a postindustrial future. The essay is a lucid account of lived moments of the author and her struggle for perspective as a "home maker", where she dexterously tries to balance her sense of place, family, values, and a deep quest for knowledge. The idea of home is employed not merely as a spatial or territorial pointer, but as a receptacle that accommodates precious memories and shared values.

The author uses the term "home" interchangeably as a metaphor to mean both home as a habitat and the natural world at large. The author's idea of home ranges from the personal to the universal. Beginning from her immediate personal *oikos* to the largest circle—the planet, the author clearly states that each/all of these are dependent on each other. This view of the author is analogous to those of John Muir and the bioregionalist Gene Marshall. According to Marshall (1993), the full meaning of "home" is all of these circles. He writes, "I stand at one point in space which is inside all of these circles. None of these circles can be neglected, and all are dependent on each other" (p. 56). Shepard's peregrinations map both her lived geography and her subjective–experiential engagement (Thoreauvian) informed by a deep ecological consciousness.

As an inhabitant of a distinctly different geophysical space—India (which the author refers to several times in the piece) the essay reminds me of the concept of *Tinai*—a bioregional idea in Indian literature and Tamil literature in particular (Tamil being an ancient Dravidian Language spoken in Southern India). Indian literature and Tamil literature in particular, speaks of a "'primal society', *Tinai* that preceded the stratified caste society of the Tamils" (Selvamony, 2004, p.3). The land-based society or *Tinai* is documented in the pre-Christian Tamil texts and is based on the principles of ecological egalitarianism: An all inclusive society that encompasses human beings, organisms, and ecosystems alike. The ancient Tamils identified four basic types of society based on scrubland, mountains, plains around freshwater sources and the sea coast: traditionally named as *Mullai, Kurunji, Marutam, Neytal* and *Pallai. Tinai,* which is more than a mere discourse of place, integrates the "natural, the cultural and the sacred" (Selvamony, 2003, p. 314). It is this understanding of the *oikos* as a space for ecological integration which is also perhaps the central argument of Dr.Shepard's essay.

References

Marshall,G. (1993) *Boundaries of home: Mapping for local empowerment.* Philadelphia: New Society Publishers.

Selvamony, N. (2003). Oikopoetics with special reference to Tamil poetry. In S.J. Lawrence & K. Bhagavati (Eds.), *Tamilogical Research Ideas: Literature* (pp. 314–322). Chennai, India: International Institute of Tamil Studies.

Selvamony, N. (2004). Tinai studies. (Tinai, 3). Chennai, India: Persons for Alternative Social Order.

VIDYA SARVESWARAN is presently a PhD scholar with the Department of Humanities and Social Sciences at the Indian Institute of Technology Madras (IIT Madras). She works in the field of Literature and Environment with a special reference to the literary works of the American writer Terry Tempest Williams. Ms. Sarveswaran was a Fulbright Fellow with the University of Nevada, Reno, for the year 2009–2009. Her research interests include American, British and Indian Literature, Literature and the Environment, Deep Ecology, Drama, Film studies and Creative Writing.

The Pooh Hypothesis: A Response

Michael Caley

Calely, M. (2011). The Pooh hypothesis: A Response. *Restoration Earth: An Interdisciplinary Journal for the Study of Nature & Civilization*, *1*(1), 43–49. Copyright © The Authors. All rights reserved. For reprint information contact: oceanseminary@verizon.net.

Abstract

A theory to address the seeming inability of humans to solve ecological, social, political and economic problems is presented: After 8000 years of self-domestication humans become morphologically and behaviorally neotenic. Most humans, individually and collectively, now exhibit juvenile or adolescent behaviors that actively and passively prevent the solution of complex social, economic, political and environmental problems.

Key words: neoteny, domestication, juvenile, adolescent, adult, Pooh

Introduction

"If people were Superior to Animals they'd take better care of the world", said Pooh.
(Hoff, 1982, *The Tao of Pooh*, p. 77)

My colleague and wonderful friend, Rangarajan Swarnalatha asked me, early in 2010, to write a paper for the 2011 issue of the *Indian Journal of Eco-criticism*. At about the same time, Mark A. Schroll, Guest Managing Editor of *Anthropology of Consciousness*, *22*(1), 2011, asked me to write a "response" to a paper submitted by Alan Drengson ("Shifting Paradigms: from Technocrat to Planetary Person" personal communication). The response had to be 600–700 words and was written in April 2010.

At the time I started writing this paper I was approaching my 65th birthday. Reflecting, as I tried to develop the 600-word response for Mark into a full paper for Swarna, I realized that my life has been a search for answers to two questions. The first question is, "What does it mean to be human?" A corollary to that question is, "How does an individual achieve that?" As an adolescent, I would not have phrased the question that way, but the quest for an answer has been at least 50 years in the journeying. Much too long, I suspect.

The second question arises from my avocation as a natural historian. I am formally educated in zoology, evolutionary biology and science education. Since I first read Rachel Carson's *Silent Spring* decades ago, I have been puzzled by the seeming inability of humans to stop ongoing ecological destruction. We are the only species that destroys ecosystems with the knowledge that we are doing so, the knowledge of how not to do so, and yet we continue to do so. As Pooh Bear asserts, humans do not "take better care of the world".

My response to Alan Drengson's paper was an attempt to address this dilemma. As I sought to develop those ideas further, I realized that I had subtly missed the mark. I had suggested that we continue on our destruction of ecosystems and each other because we have become individually and collectively insane as a result of increasing population density. We carry on as if doing insane things is normal and call it "progress". I have realized that the problem is much deeper.

Neoteny and Behavioral Change

Polymorphism is the existence of two or more phenotypes in a population. Blood type, in humans, is a polymorphism. This trait is not discrete and exists in varying percentages of the genotype. Polymorphisms can be found in almost all populations organisms. The red fox, *Vulpes vulpes*, is a small canid found in the northern hemisphere. It has three distinct polymorphisms: red, cross and silver. The relative percentages of the three phases are function of population density. In low population density the predominant phase is red. As population density increases, the cross phase increases and then at very high densities the silver phase increases, as a percentage of the total population.

Each phase shows different morphological and behavioral characteristics. Many of the behavioral characteristics may be measured in terms of approachability. The red phase foxes are solitary as adults and difficult to approach, even in captivity. The cross phase is more approachable and the silver phase is very approachable. In terms of increasing population density, each phase can tolerate increasing numbers of interactions with other adult foxes. This presumably enhances survival when population density is high.

When I began my M.Sc. program at the University of Alaska, my supervisor, R. Dale Guthrie, was in the midst of a multi-year study on red fox population density and phenotypic change. The study was funded by an NSF grant. Dale purchased fox carcasses from trappers throughout Alaska, that arrived at the lab frozen. We thawed the carcasses, weighed and measured them, then autopsied them for gastric and intestinal ulcers, adrenal gland weight and eye lens weight. At that time, these were considered to be indicators of stress in mammals. We found statistically significant changes in these stress indicators in each of the phases. Red foxes showed higher levels of stress, cross foxes lower levels, and silver foxes still lower levels.

Other studies on phenotypic variation in *Vulpes vulpes* have been carried out by Belyaev (Trut 1999). Belyaev and his colleagues selected for approachability in captive *Vulpes vulpes* populations for 40 generations. His adult foxes were easily tamed, exhibited puppy-play behavior, and were morphological neotenic with floppy ears, shortened muzzles and domed foreheads—and were all silver phase.

As humans began to tame and then domesticate wild animals, the first trait to be noticed and selected would have been some kind of docility. Approach/avoidance distances vary between individuals in every population. Those animals that allow closer approach are easier to trap and tame. Selecting for that trait alone is sufficient to create the cascade of other traits.

All mammals, as newborns, must be approachable by their mothers and must be able to approach their mothers. Approachability must be a juvenile trait, especially in mammal species that have multiple births. The variability of approachability can be selected, naturally or artificially. However, selection never affects single traits only. The genome is completely connected, it is recursive and, we now know that there are powerful epigenetic forces that impact on selection perturbations (Jablonka & Lamb, 2005). As far as I can determine, all domesticated species show greater or lesser degrees of neoteny.

Self-Selection in Human Populations

In forty generations Belyaev, selecting for only one trait, approachibility, produced foxes that were morphologically and behaviorally neotenic. Humans in settlements, experience selection pressures not found in small foraging groups and such selection pressures favor domestication. We have been self-selecting for behavioral traits that allow us to live in larger and larger groups for more than 8,000 years. We know that settlements of more than 250 have been found as long as ago as 8,000 years BCE. With an average generation length of twenty-five years, we have been domesticating and neotenizing ourselves for more than 300 generations—many more than Belyaev's forty generations of foxes.

What Does It Mean To Be Human?

My question expands to this: "What are the characteristics of an fully functioning adult human being?" I have realized only lately that I am now able to answer that question. Before I do so, I feel compelled to tell you more about myself.

I am old enough to remember when the terms "natural history" and "natural historian" had both meaning and cachet in the general population. You seldom hear these terms any more. As an adolescent I read the books of Ray Chapman Andrews, Lowell Thomas, Henry Hudson, Charles Darwin, and many others. Although I lived in a large metropolis, my friends and I had access to relatively unsettled rural wild areas, which we frequented as often as possible. I knew very early that I would be involved in the biological sciences; and, beginning in 1965, I subsequently acquired university degrees in Zoology, Evolutionary Biology, and Science Education.

Thirty years ago, I began to learn the Chinese arts of Taijiquan and Qigong. I have played these arts ever since and I have read broadly and deeply in the literature of Daoism and Chan (Zen). That interest has been supported, in the past decade, with the very kind aid of an amazing scholar of classical Chinese philosophy, Roger T. Ames (University of Hawai'i). If not for the detailed explications of what Roger and his colleague David Hall term the *wu-forms*, I would not have been able to delineate my hypothesis (Table 1). The *wu-forms* define the living goal of Daoist adepts (sages) and have done so for at least 3,000 years. Combining deep introspection of an individual life with the embodiment of the *wu-forms* through intense body awareness (Taijiquan, Qigong, Yoga, etc) seems to me to define at least one path to adulthood. Interestingly, for generation upon generation, Daoists have followed the WAY by leaving settlements and trekking into the mountains of China. As the saying goes, "Cloud hidden, whereabout unknown".

WU-FORMS	Standard Translation	Ames & Hall (2003) transliteration
Wu wei	No action	Non-coercive action
Wu zhi	No knowledge	Unprincipled knowing
Wu yu	No desire	Objectless desire
Wu shi	No business	Non interfering in daily business
Wu xin	No mind	Unmediated thinking & feeling
Wu zheng	No striving	Striving without contention
Wu ming	Nameless	Designating without prejudice

Table 1

Over the past decades, I have also followed my deepening interest in human evolution, especially that of anatomically modern humans. It is in the intersection of modern biological theory, Daoist philosophy, and qi practice that my understanding of what it means to be an adult human emerged. Some of these ideas have been explored in previous publications (see Caley, 1987, 2009).

Homo sapiens Version 1.0.

Just as dogs have evolved from their wolf ancestors (i.e., dogs are not wolves), humans in most of the world have evolved from our Pleistocene ancestors. Version 1.0 of modern humans was the ultimate forager (and a very few have survived, pushed into remote or marginal living areas, where they continue to live as they have for more than 30,000 years). Our Paleolithic ancestors were generally taller than modern humans with much more robust skeletons and musculature. Worldwide humans have in the last 10,000 years become smaller and more gracile. (Taylor, 2010; Wade, 2006) There is little evidence of caries, diabetes, arthritis, or many other diseases. They had larger brains. They colonized and adapted to every niche from equatorial jungles and deserts to the high arctic and from sea level to high altitude. Adult males and females had encyclopedic knowledge of the landforms, geologic conditions, plants and animals, and of the seasonal changes of the territory they roamed (Guthrie, 2005). Our ancestors were very versatile and skilled. They made all of their implements and clothing from locally obtained materials. Stone blades (from a variety of materials), scrapers and awls (from stone, wood, and bone) were and are as efficient as modern steel and ceramic tools. Women made tailored clothes from tanned skins.

From burial sites, it is evident that they were ceremonial humans who connected across generations. The typical group was about thirty people in all ages from newborns to elders with some individuals living into forties or fifties. The births of children were spaced about four years apart with breastfeeding continuing until age four or five. They reached physical maturity, as do we, in their teens; cognitive maturity, as do we, in their twenties; and emotional maturity in their thirties. As far as we can determine they lived full lives, with minimum work and maximum socialization. (Guthrie, 2005)

Each forager group would have been in periodic, perhaps annual, contact with about ten other groups in the local area. Territories ranged from perhaps 100- to 500-square miles, depending upon the density of plants and animals. This upper limit of about 300 contacts in any individual's life appears, at least to me, to be critical in the development of fully adult humans. (Guthrie, 2005) Barker and Gump (1964) demonstrated that in American Mid-West high schools, populations of students greater than about 250 spontaneously split into smaller groups, with which students identified.

The Neotenization of *Homo sapiens*

When there were only ancestral humans on the planet, there was little or no need for self-domestication and its unintended consequence, neotenization. Individuals lived full lives, became functional adults, passed knowledge to succeeding generations and perhaps became revered elders. With the advent of settlements greater than 250 individuals, it became necessary to domesticate humans along with other animals and plants. Humans were forced from their natural HOME into the *wilds* of the *urbs* and the *domus*. Domestication required that selection favor the most accommodating and docile individuals for living in *unnaturally* large populations. These juvenile and adolescent traits, as we have seen, are now maintained into adulthood. This can be seen especially in female humans. Retention of childlike traits of large eyes, small chin, rounded head, reduced body, and childlike gait has become the norm in most developed societies. The recent trend to removing all body hair from physically mature humans is also a form of neotenization. Further modern women frequently use cosmetics and surgery to emphasize childlike characteristics, routinely wear clothing that creates the illusion of youthful bodies, and also wear high heels that changes their gait to childlike prancing. It could also be suggested the ultimate in the neotenization of women may be the practice of foot binding (although now largely absent) of Chinese women and the Muslim *hijab*, *abaya*, and *chador* used to cover women. Foot binding makes a woman unable to walk properly or far thus maintaining a childlike gait and dependency; while the full robes required in *some* Muslim communities may make women almost unrecognizable as human and could be read as symbolic of a return to the anonymity of the womb.

We see further examples of the neotinization of women in Japan through *manga* and *hentai*, which create adolescent pornography for physical adults with adolescent fantasies. The female characters are adolescent sex fantasies with huge eyes, tiny waists, improbable breasts and buttocks. While in the West, women action heroes show similar characteristics. Adolescent drives of "sex, drugs and rock and roll" became the mantra of the late twentieth century continuing through the emergence of rap music. Rock, pop, and rap videos have taken adolescent sexual fantasies *ad absurdum*.

The Qualia of Adult Humans

The following list is not in any particular order. The qualia represent my understanding of adultness. It is important to realize that the list is not exhaustive and other language may be used to express similar ideas and concepts. It is also important to realize that English, like many other languages, forces a linearity to understanding that does not accurately reflect the thinking/doing experience. These qualia have emerged, over many years, from the concatenation of my personal experience and the knowledge I have received from many sources, some adults included. The qualia are *all-or-nothing*—a gestalt.

- Embracing both silence and paradox
- Living non-coercively, non-contentiously, and non-interferingly
- Unmediated thinking/feeling/doing emerging from introspective meditation
- Loving unconditionally
- Living with sufficiency
- Cooperating as the fundamental basis of living
- Living unprincipled, amoral, and responsible lives (see Moeller, 2009)
- Living without fearing death
- Not killing other humans, except *in extremis* (see Grossman, 2009)
- Living ceremoniously

On The Necessity of Adolescence

Lest the reader think that I am a grumpy, cantankerous or curmudgeonly old man who has forgotten his own youth or who looks back to some golden age, let me say that adolescence, along with infancy and childhood are necessary periods of human development. Individuals and societies fail when one period is given precedence over all others. Golding's (1954) *The Lord of the Flies* is a horrid testimony to the unlimited rule of adolescence. The curious, eager, inquisitive, exuberant, outgoing, and vital qualities of adolescents are apparent wherever they are. Adolescents believe themselves to be invincible and without limit. The bands of humans who walked out of Africa 50,000 years ago were doubtlessly led by adolescents. Adolescents probably led humans, crossing from Beringia to Alaska 15,000 years ago. For millennia, Australian Aboriginal adolescents have been going walk-about. The historically rapid peopling of North and South America was the result of the explorations of adolescents. Adolescents likely paddled the ocean going canoes used to people Polynesia. The throwing spear and the atlatl were probably invented by adolescents, but perfected by adults with more experience in working wood and stone. The development of the bow and arrow probably followed a similar path. It is adolescents who try to break boundaries and that is absolutely necessary for the continuation of the human species.

My response to Pooh Bear's Hypothesis
"If people were Superior to Animals they'd take better care of the world", said Pooh.

This is a wonderfully parsed hypothesis. The "if, then" aspect is explicit. The "truth" of the first part is dependent upon the "truth" of the second part. It follows; therefore, that since people do not take better care of the world, they are not superior animals. No other animal routinely destroys its environment; many modify their environments, but no other routinely destroys it. Since the development of settlements and agriculture, humans, globally, have destroyed their local environments. (Diamond, 2005)

As for taking better care of the world, only adults can take care of children, adolescents, and the world. Adolescents, in every culture known, *are taken care of*; they are not caretakers. Unfortunately, most humans no longer have the opportunity to become adults. The majority of those who appear to be physically mature humans are behaviorally adolescents or even juveniles. Just listen to the words and observe that actions of the people who have assumed political, economic, or religious power in our world. You will perceive neither the words nor the actions of psychologically or emotionally mature adults.

Adolescents are characterized by immature emotions and desires. Adolescents do not recognize limits. For adolescents enough is never enough and the world is dichotomous—black/white, right/wrong, good/evil, etc. The greed of the financial markets, the opposition of conservatives and liberals (Democrats and Republicans), and the adherence to fundamentalist political, social, economic, and religious ideologies are all examples of adolescent behavior.

Adolescents are incapable of taking better care of the world because they are emotionally immature. Remember, after the collapse of the World Trade Centre in New York on September 11, 2001, President Bush announced to the world, "You are either with us or against us!" In his adolescent fantasies he perceived of himself, I suspect, as an American superhero that would save the world from tyrants. The wars in Iraq and Afghanistan continue, unabated, years later. His fundamentalist opponents *also* show the characteristic behavior of adolescents. Local, national and international politics and economics are reminiscent of the arguments of twelve-year-old boys, but with much more dire consequences.

This theory suggests that the majority of humans now are functionally adolescent resulting in social, political, economic, and environmental instabilities that cannot be adapted to nor solved through adolescent behavior. Since the majority of the humans now have few adult role models and since humans learn best by imitation and since there are insufficient adults to imitate there is (are) now no group(s) of humans large enough "to take better care of the world".

If this is a robust theory, it must do, at least two things: (a) it must account for the data under consideration; and (b) it must suggest other ways of supporting or refuting itself. The theory offers a testable account for the problem of why humans are unable to solve many complex social, political, and environmental problems. The theory suggests that examining the words and actions of political, social, economic and religious leaders may demonstrate that they are the words and actions of juveniles and adolescents, rather than adults.

References

Ames, R. T., & Hall, D. L. (2003). *DaoDeJing: a philosophical translation*. New York: Ballantine Books.

Barker, R., & Gimp, P. (1964). *Big School, small school: high school size and student behavior*. San Francisco: Stanford University Press.

Caley, M. T. (1987). Taoist musings on Ecosophosophy and change. *The Trumpeter*, 4(2), 21–22.

Caley, M. T. (2009). Some thoughts on Wu-forms and autopoiesis. *The Indian Journal of Eco-Criticism*, 1(1), 65–75.

Diamond, J. (2005). *Collapse: how societies choose to fail or succeed*. New York: Penguin Books.

Golding, W. (1954). *The Lord of the flies*. United Kingdom: Faber and Faber.

Grossman, D. (2009). *On killing: The psychological cost of learning to kill in war and society* (revised edition). New York: Back Bay Book.

Guthrie, R. D. (2005). *The nature of Paleolithic art*. Chicago: University of Chicago Press.

Hoff, B. (1983). *The Tao of Pooh*. New York: Penguin Paperbacks.

Jablonka, E., & Lamb, M. (2005). *Four dimensions for evolution*. Boston: MIT Press.

Moeller, H-G. (2009). *The moral fool: a case for amorality.* New York: Columbia University Press.

Taylor, T. (2010). *The artificial ape: How technology changed the course of human evolution.* New York: Palgrave Macmillan.

Trut, L. N. (1999). Early canid domestication: The fox farm experiment. *American Scientist, 87,* 160–169.

Wade, N. (2006). *Before the dawn.* New York: Penguin Books.

Note: Shortly after submitting this article to the IJE, I was informed that the IJE was being taken, peremptorily, from Dr. Rangarajan and the Indian Institute of Technology to a newly formed Indian University somewhere in a rural area. The whole Editorial Board was dismissed and a new Board is presumably being created.

MICHAEL T. CALEY is an peripatetic scholar, surviving employment in academe, government, public education and the private sector. He is currently the Editor-in-Chief of *The Trumpeter: A Journal of Ecosophy.* He is also a 30 year player/teacher of Chinese *Qi* arts—*Taijiquan, Ba Duan Jin* and *Qi Gong.* Often found wandering effortlessly in the Dao, he frequently appears to be simply lazy, to his great delight.

"Bones" copyright © 2010 by Katherine Batten MacDowell. Photo taken at Sandy Hook, New Jersey. From *A Study of Sandy Hook..*

Sufi Wisdom, Norse Mythology, Zen Koans, and the Eco-Crisis: Remembering the Value of Teaching-Stories

Mark A. Schroll

Schroll, M.A. (2011). Sufi wisdom, Norse mythology, Zen koans, and the eco-crisis: Remembering the value of teaching-stories. *Restoration Earth: An Interdisciplinary Journal for the Study of Nature & Civilization, 1*(1), 50–61. Copyright © The Authors. All rights reserved. For reprint information contact: ocean-seminary@verizon.net.

All our dazzling computer technology seems to have increased actual work time in the U.S. rather than reduced it. . . . Yet peoples commonly labeled as hunters and gatherers seem to have worked three to fifteen hours per week—enough time to self-actualize with stories, crafts, ceremonies, love-making, ecstasies, and so forth.
(Kremer, 2002, p. 17)

In a sprawl smart house, no level of conspicuous consumption is directly related to your bank balance.
(Firesign Theatre, 1999)

Introduction

Critics of this article will be correct in pointing out the contradiction of criticizing the erosion of human-kind's quality of life via technology as I write this on a computer using artificial lighting, then sending it to be edited, and making its publication available using the Internet, all of which are powered by electricity. Thus to clarify, it is not technology I am calling into question; instead it is the influence on our approach to knowing that has resulted in the cultural manifestation that Theodore Roszak referred to as *technocracy* (Roszak, 1969, 1973). The importance of Roszak's contribution was called back into my awareness as I edited Alan Drengson's (2011) article "Shifting Paradigms: From Technocrat to Planetary Person", who provides us with a clear definition of technocracy as well as its stark influence on our lives. "Technocracy", as Drengson points out:

> Carried to its logical end it *seeks to turn the world into a controlled and manipulated artifact*. Nature is only a resource to be processed. This process in turn becomes self-perpetuating and self justifying; and in time it must also bring human social activities under technological control. This in turn involves behavioral technology and social engineering. Humans must now be "designed" to fit the technological mold and matrix, since they are fallible in their normal form, and they might disrupt the technological and economic processes. (Drengson, p. 15)

In essence, "conformity is our commodity" (Schroll, 2005, p. 61)—packaged, processed, and programmed.

In support of this introduction's critique, and in opposition to the dominant discourses promoting technocracy, this article's thesis argues that teaching stories—specifically Sufi wisdom, Norse mythology, and Zen koans—offer paths toward remembering other ways of knowing, and that these ways of knowing provide us with a countercultural antidote to the technocratic influences on our way of being. In more precise terms, teaching stories offer us multilevel strategies of meta-analysis as a means of freeing our consciousness from immersion in a media-saturated cultural environment that is so pervasive it makes our criticism of it seem to be a symptom of madness. We are assisted in this meta-analysis with the healing antidote of the Sufi story "When the Waters Were Changed":

Once upon a time Khidr, the Teacher of Moses, called upon mankind with a warning. At a certain date, he said, all the water in the world which had not been specially hoarded would disappear. It would then be renewed, with different water, which would drive men mad. Only one man listened to the meaning of this advice. He collected water and went to a secure place where he stored it, and waited for the water to change its character.

On the appointed date the streams stopped running, the wells went dry, and the man who had listened, seeing this happening, went to his retreat and drank his preserved water. When he saw, from his security, the waterfalls again beginning to flow, this man descended among the other sons of men. He found that they were thinking and talking in an entirely different way from before; yet they had no memory of what had happened; nor of having been warned. When he tried to talk to them, he realized that they thought he was mad, and they showed hostility or compassion, not understanding.

At first he drank none of the new water, but went back to his concealment, to draw on his supplies, every day. Finally, however, he took the decision to drink the new water because he could not bear the loneliness of living, believing and thinking in a different way from everyone else. He drank the new water, and became like the rest. Then he forgot all about his own store of special water, and his fellows began to look upon him as a madman who had miraculously been restored to sanity. (Shah, 1970, p. 21)

Cultural Amnesia and Scientism

My interpretation of the above Sufi story is that the "water" being talked about is a metaphor for consciousness. Khidr's warning to hoard "special water" is a metaphor that represents ancestral wisdom grounded in experiential knowing of transpersonal states. The "new water" is a metaphor representing technocracy's influence on our way of being. Moreover I believe the pervasive influence of technocracy has existed in one form or another in many cultures since the emergence of tool use (a hypothesis worthy of its own research to clearly document) (see Batteau, 2010; Drengson, 1995; Fromm, 1968). Thus the act of drinking the new water represents our loss of ancestral wisdom, it represents a loss of what Huston Smith calls the "primordial tradition" (Smith, 1976; Schroll, in press), and it represents what I have referred to as *cultural amnesia* (Schroll, 1988). I argue:

> . . . that many of the so-called "facts" we use to construct our paradigm are not "facts" at all, but socially constructed shared assumptions, [an unconscious infrastructure of ideas], becoming "hypnotized" by consensus reality and begin acting toward our cultural assumptions as "social facts," which later manifest themselves as social psychological pressures (Schroll, 1988, p. 317–318).

A year after my chapter was published the phrase "cultural amnesia" was used in a similar fashion in Paul Devereux, John Steel, and David Kubrin's book *Earthmind: A Modern Adventure in Ancient Wisdom* (Devereux, Steel, & Kubrin, 1989, p. 123), showing that we were both independently thinking along similar lines.

Also very similar to cultural amnesia, yet more specifically focused on science, is what Charles T. Tart tells us is referred to as *scientism*:

> I was recently credited with coining the word *scientism*, but this is not true. Back in the early 19th century, sociologists were talking about *scientism* when they recognized that for a lot of scientists, the practice of science was no longer a method for trying to refine our knowledge about reality. It became an arrogant agenda where we basically figured out everything important and we could ignore all of the worldviews that did not fit (Tart, 2009, p. 6).

Thus scientism (which continues to limit the actual practice of science), cultural amnesia, and technocracy may all be considered similar in their meaning and equally responsible for the cultural malaise, which wandering dervishes have whispered about in tea houses for centuries in the Middle East and re-told as Sufi stories. These murmurs of discontent also found voices of expression in Russian authors, such as Yevgeny Zamyatin's novel *We* (written between 1920–1921) (Zamyatin, 1972). *We*, like the more well known novels *Brave New World* by Aldous Huxley (1932/1969) and George Orwell's *1984* (1949), provides vivid portrayals of social engineering that Roszak aptly summed up and referred to as technocracy. All of these examples represent the variety of influences that have come together to form the resistance movement that Roszak called *the counter culture*.

The Counter Culture: Remembering Other Ways of Knowing

In his 1989 book *Imaginary Landscape: Making Worlds of Myth and Science*, William Irwin Thompson suggests one of the reasons scientists, philosophers, and people from all walks of life have become fascinated with the "narration's of world formation" and cosmology is a direct consequence of modernity's social fabric coming apart at the seams. Thompson's assessment continues to be a relevant description as the 21st century unfolds. Echoing into this century are the counter culture's cries of concern that find expression through Internet conversations I have with people on every continent. One of the many ways I have expressed both my existential anxiety and a need to connect with others who share my concern about wanting to create a better world is through my poem "I'm an Alien (Youth)" (1997):

Nobody asked if I wanted to be born here.
I'm tired of feeling like an uninvited guest.
Stop trying to steal my individuality.
Stop trying to transform me into something
That you can understand. Stop trying to change me.
Because I am here waiting in this city, and other cities like it
Wandering and searching for others like myself.
Being driven mad by the silence.
Being driven mad by the loneliness.
Being driven mad by the confinement.
Bored and driven to the streets
Seeking to satisfy the aching and the hunger for communication.
Feeling dissected, feeling disrespected, feeling disconnected.
I'm an alien, I'm an alien, I'm an alien (an alien youth).
I'm searching for a place that I can call home.

This search for home, a way to make sense of modernity's social fabric coming apart at the seams and our reaching out for a sense of direction, was addressed by Thompson (1986) in his book *Pacific Shift*. He wryly asks: "Is the human being simply a catalytic agent secreted by Gaia to transform the subterranean oceans of oil into a moving gas in the earth's atmosphere?" (p. 74). This brainteaser is Thompson's effort to awaken our unconscious as an ally for paradigmatic change; he points out cultural transformations are not "registered" and reported on a conscious level, instead they find a resonance within us through the mythos of a culture and its artists. The point Thompson is making: we find ourselves facing the eco-crises *not* because technocracy has failed us, but rather facing the crises because of its success. Thompson argues (paraphrasing Gregory Bateson) that missing from this technocratic agenda is "the pattern that connects….the personal pattern of friendship, as well as the larger cultural pattern of transformation" (p. 73). In particular, this article seeks to assist our ability to register with the deeper sense of wisdom within us through the use of Sufi stories; Norse mythology, Zen koans, and other related literary mediums.

Echoing the sentiments expressed in my poem, Charlene Spretnak (1991) eloquently sums up our present situation in her book *States of Grace*, telling us:

The spirit of modernity shed the wisdom traditions [some call them the great religions, the perennial philosophy, or the primordial tradition—] in whatever society it took root because of faith that the truth of "value-free" science and the power of technology would break new ground in social well-being and carry along in its momentum, ethics, morality, and culture—all remade according to the impetus of progress. . . . The assumptions of that worldview have led us to widespread ecocide, nuclear arms, the globalization of unqualified-growth economies, and the plunder of Third and Fourth World (indigenous) peoples' cultures and homelands. The psychological costs have been heavy, as well: loss of meaning beyond consumerism, loss of community and connectedness with other people, and loss of a secure sense of embeddedness in the rest of the natural world. (p. 3–4)

Spretnak's perspective of immeasurable loss through our present worldview is embodied in the character Sonja Hoffman (played by Liv Ullman in Fritjof Capra's film *Mindwalk* [1991]) as she says, "What we need is a new vision of the world." This need for a new vision of the world is the need for a new world interpretation, a new world orientation, in other words, a new worldview or *mythos* (Schroll, 2011).

The Greek word *mythos* means telling a tale. Thus we are searching for a new way of speaking, a new way of telling our stories, a new way of framing our questions (Tart, 2009). Using the word mythos in this way allows us to find a sense of common ground with storytelling. According to Elaine Wynne (1987): "If we want to change the way that other people think about us, and the way that other people treat us, the first step is to use our imagination to change our stories" (p. 482). Story in this sense refers to our own inner voice, our personal narrative, the things we tell ourselves about our life and the lives of others. Utilizing the construct of mythos as Wynne articulates not only allows us to re-conceptualize our cultural stories and how people treat each other at the broadest of levels, but it allows us to:

1. Reinvent our individual selves, because our lives are made up of stories. To transform our self into the kind of person we want to be. Wynne explains, "stories are the glue, the essence that holds a people together . . . a family, a community, a nation, a planet" (p. 486). Deena Metzger (1992) neatly sums up the importance of storytelling toward the creation and maintenance of a healthy personality, thereby creating and maintaining a coherent culture, by reminding us: "Stories heal us because we become whole through them. . . . We restore those parts of ourselves that have been scattered, hidden, suppressed, denied, distorted, forbidden" (quoted in Glendinning, 1994, p. 146).

2. Point us towards the importance of visionary experience, because visions tell us about our future. Visions give us inspiration and hope (Schroll, 2007).

The practice and importance of storytelling has, however, become a lost art within our Euro–American scientific worldview; which has become so completely focused on the rational, intellectual process of analysis that we have forgotten the importance of Eros as a way of knowing.[1] The importance and value of other ways of knowing—knowing from multiple perspectives—is illustrated in the Sufi story, "Never Know When It Might Come in Useful":

> Nasrudin sometimes took people for trips in his boat. One day a pedagogue hired him to ferry him across a very wide river. As soon as they were afloat, the scholar asked whether it was going to be rough. "Don't ask me nothing about it," Nasrudin said. "Have you never studied grammar?" "No," said the Mulla. "In that case, half your life has been wasted." The Mulla said nothing. Soon a terrible storm blew up. The Mulla's crazy cockleshell was filling with water. He leaned over toward his companion. "Have you ever learned to swim?" "No," said the pedant. "In that case, schoolmaster, all your life is lost for we are sinking." (Ornstein, 1972, p. 49)

One of the best summaries describing storytelling's importance as a way of knowing and perceiving from a multiplicity of perspectives and domains of consciousness has been written by Idris Shah (1968), whose thoughts on this are worth quoting at length:

> The teaching-story was brought to perfection as a communication instrument many thousand years ago. The fact that it has not developed greatly since then has caused people obsessed by some theories of our current civilizations to regard it as the product of a less enlightened time. They feel that it must surely be little more than a literary curiosity, something fit for children, the projection, perhaps of infantile desires, a means of enacting a wish-fulfillment. Hardly anything could be further from the truth of such pseudo-philosophical, certainly unscientific, imaginings…. So little is known to the academics, the scholars and the intellectuals of this world about these materials, that there is no word in modern languages which has been set aside to describe them…
>
> Real teaching-stories are not to be confused with parables; which are adequate enough in their intention, but still on a lower level of material, generally confined to the inculcation of moralistic principles, not the assistance of interior movement of the human mind. Unlike the parable, the meaning of the teaching-story cannot be unraveled by ordinary intellectual methods alone…. The closest that we can come to describing its effect is to say that it connects with part of the individual which cannot

---

[1]See Batten (MacDowell) and Schroll, 2011, this volume for a definition of Eros, and its relationship and differentiation from Logos.

be reached by any convention, and that it establishes in him or her a means of communication with a non-verbalized truth beyond the customary limitations of our familiar dimensions. (p. 95–96)

In resume, this brings us to a clear and simple means of describing the importance of the process and benefits of finding our path to the transpersonal, or to what Shah has referred to as the "non-verbalized truth beyond the customary limitations of our familiar dimensions." In other words, this is the relevance of inviting this knowledge into our conscious awareness so that we can create the kind of place we want the world to be and the kind of self we wish to become. This brings us back to the bulleted points we discussed earlier about how stories impact the self. The Zen story, or Zen koan,[2] "What Are You Doing, What Are You Saying" illustrates this point that, while important as a memory device, our reliance on any text as a primary source of enlightened vision is really a hindrance to our ability to directly experience the transpersonal:

> The Zen master Mu-nan had only one successor. His name was Shoju. After Shoju had completed his study of Zen, Mu-nan called him into his room. "I am getting old," he said, "and as far as I know, Shoju, you are the only one who will carry on this teaching. Here is a book. It has been passed down from master to master for seven generations. I have added many points according to my understanding. The book is very valuable, and I am giving it to you to represent your successorship."
>
> "If the book is such an important thing, you had better keep it," Shoju replied. "I received your Zen without writing and am satisfied with it as it is."
>
> "I know that," said Mu-nan. "Even so, this work has been carried from master to master for seven generations, so you may keep it as a symbol of having received the teaching. Here."
>
> They happened to be talking before a brazier. The instant Shoju felt the book in his hands he thrust it into the flaming coals. He had no lust for possessions.
>
> Mu-nan, who never had been angry before, yelled: "What are you doing!"
>
> Shoju shouted back: "What are you saying!" (Reps, 1998, p. 80–81)

Likewise another way of viewing the intended meaning of this Zen story is to say it is a means of clearing up the confusion between symbol and reality, as Alan W. Watts (1970) points out: "the peculiar and perhaps fatal fallacy of civilization [is] the confusion of symbol and reality. . . . All too easily, we confuse the world as we symbolize it with the world as it is. As semanticist Alfred Korzybski used say, it is an urgent necessity to distinguish the map and the territory" (p. 5). This too is a description of both the path and the relevance of cultivating the transpersonal perspective. Similarly it is important to clarify that myths, metaphors, and storytelling are what preserve or keep alive the transpersonal perspective in our daily lives. Reiterating once again, this is what I mean by an act of remembering to become whole. The full process of how I have hypothesized we cultivate the transpersonal exceeds this article's limits and has been taken up in Schroll (2010) and Schroll (in press).

Transpersonal Ecosophy's Relationship to Indigenous Wisdom

> *What no home now?*
> *It's not the same.*
> *It's not there anymore.*
> *Don't know who the fuck to blame.*
> *They say that home is where the heart is.*
> *What do you do when it's been ripped in two?*
> *They say that home is where the heart is.*
> *When you've got nothing what would you do?*
> *What would you do if I were you?*
> (Tim Masters, 1998)

---

[2] Earnest Wood (1957) defines a *koan* as:

> An exercise for the mind, beyond thought, presented by a Zen Master, and of such a nature that it violates the postulates of logic. It is as though one should be presented with a canvas on which many different marks had been made together at random and were asked: "What is the meaning of this?". . . . In a secondary way the koan is a kind of test of the enquirer's enlightenment, since he may or may not "catch on," and show in some way that the koan has had immediate effect (p. 65 & 67).

Whenever I listen to Tim Masters's song "Home", my imagination creates scenes of war-torn nations, shattered families, broken relationships, people struggling for social justice, and the need to remember my own fragmented genealogical origins. Jurgen W. Kremer (2000) sums up this loss of home in his article "Millennial Twins: An Essay into Time and Place", whose thoughts on this matter are worth repeating:

> Since the middle of the 2nd millennium, we find an increasing prevalence of what is now called ethnic cleansing. The murderous forces, which were in large part Christian-church dominated, perpetuated genocide not just against indigenous peoples in other countries but against the holders of indigenous knowledge within their own boundaries, including women who were killed in witchhunts. Genocide in the service of the Eurocentered story continues relentlessly planetwide, primarily through the various forms of economic globalization, also known as Americanization (the destruction of sustainable economies and the creation of dependency in the name of progress and civilization). While we may be tempted to soften the shock of this process by calling it cultural genocide, it can be considered to be the genocide of cultures and cultural identities. People are murdered as the indigenous persons they are, even though they may resurrect themselves as persons of Eurocentered minds. Pervasive ecocide and sexism are corollaries to this story. (p. 33)

In an attempt to begin healing this genocide (see Schroll & Walker, 2001), Kremer (2000) reminds us of the essential importance that remembering the indigenous names of places, plants, and stories of all cultures has upon our psyche. Kremer points out that it has been humankind's cultural amnesia of this indigenous wisdom that has created the psycho–historical space where the currently dominant social, economic, political theories, polices, and practices have been allowed to grow, thereby allowing humankind's most powerful and wealthy to feed their grub-like egos. (This is actually not a fair comparison to grubs, yet this analogy is suggesting a practice of mindless consumption for consumption sake). These gluttons (and they know who they are) live in a total state of denial about the consequences of their addiction to ever increasing profits and increasing consumption of all the life-sustaining energies of the Earth. A better analogy of this mindless consumption is the character of Galactus, the consumer of worlds in the Marvel comic *The Silver Surfer*. To survive, Galactus spends all of his time consuming the life-energies of planets throughout the universe without any thought of the consequences to whatever planet he is feeding on. Galactus's herald, the Silver Surfer, in a moment of self-transcending transpersonal awareness, realizes that the Earth and its creatures have intrinsic value and says "no" to the authority of Galactus, opposing the consumption of these life energies. This is also an example of myth providing a new worldview toward a transpersonal/ecological perspective. Meanwhile, applying this analogy to humankind's current eco-crisis, the future of planet Earth and all its creatures hang in the balance between hope and extinction, praying that the miracle of a transformation of consciousness comes in time to save us from total destruction.

Remembering Our Indigenous Pathways to Knowing and Understanding

What would our science be like if its methods of inquiry
Resembled the life-promoting rays of our sun,
As it shines onto the unopened bud of a flower,
Coaxing it to open, and unfold itself?
(Mark A. Schroll, 1995)

We can continue to think more deeply about the implications of this methodological question and our personal engagement with the transpersonal perspective with the help of the Sufi story "The Grammarian and the Dervish":

> One dark night a dervish was passing a dry well when he heard a cry for help from below. "What is the matter?" he called down. "I am a grammarian, and I have unfortunately fallen, due to my ignorance of the path, into this deep well, in which I am now all but immobilized," responded the other. "Hold friend, and I'll fetch a ladder and a rope," said the dervish. "One moment, please!" Said the

grammarian. "Your grammar and diction are faulty; be good enough to amend them." "If that is so much more important than the essentials," shouted the dervish, "you had best stay where you are until I have learned to speak properly." And he went his way. (Shah, 1970, p. 193)

Besides the recognition that humor is good medicine for healing a way of life that has gone to pieces, what is the relationship between this Sufi story and humankind's ability to remember our indigenous pathways toward knowing and understanding? Overall this story is making reference to the dark night of the scholar, which Kremer (1992) has described as ". . . a descent into the darkness and chaos thus far excommunicated from the field of legitimate inquiry" (p. 169); this descent is represented by the grammarian falling into the well. The grammarian represents the received epistemological paradigm of Euro–American science, whose analytic orientation has become so all consuming that it has become an end in itself. It is this ignorance of the epistemological path or our pathways to knowing that has resulted in the grammarian's misfortune of falling into a dry well from which he cannot escape. The dervish in this story represents those of us who are wandering through the darkness in search of *deeper and more highly integrated patterns of wholeness*. Language often reveals its limited Euclidean orientation when we seek to explore and discuss various states and stations of consciousness whose spacetime orientation is nonlocal. Therefore when I refer to "deeper," this suggests a resonance with humankind's collective unconscious and also in the shamanic sense of lower world journeys. Whereas when I refer to "higher" I am referring to progressive stages of personal development, shamanic upper world journeys, growth and evolution. Returning to the here and now, this search for wholeness is also the search for a sense of personal identity and belonging (a place to call home), the search for relationship, the search for family, and the hope of keeping a marriage together.

The grammarian is unable to free himself from the well because he refuses to abandon the quest for truth and understanding as it has been defined by Euro–American science. The grammarian represents the kind of person that refuses to believe that global climate change is a crisis and that all the nations of the world, especially the industrial nations, need to be doing something about it. People who are oriented toward the grammarian's worldview have lost sight of the essential meaning of the philosophy of science: *how does science enrich us?* Grammarians (especially those influenced by scientism and technocracy and who are suffering from cultural amnesia) seem to be oblivious to the essential problems facing us in our everyday world. Telling us that before we may begin to deal with any of these essentials we must first correct our grammar, that is, we must first demonstrate without a doubt that the scientific data being collected to support global climate change are statistically significant. Arguing from this point of view, the grammarian continues to say that the scientific data being collected to support global climate change are insignificant to the overall geological timescale.

In the meantime our continuing search for a place to call home: personal identity, belongingness, relationship, family, keeping a marriage together, and the dervish way of life is intertwined with the archetypal myth that we have been split apart. This realization that without relationship we live in a state of alienation or exile constitutes the first necessary step toward finding a true sense of community and a true sense of communion with our earth-body. Throughout our evolutionary history we have known this as our search for our lost half and the story of star-crossed lovers, such seen in the myth of Isis, Osiris, and his enemy–brother Set. Jealous of his brother's wholeness, Set cuts Osiris into pieces and scatters the fragments of his dismembered body all over the world. Coming to his rescue, Isis sets out on a quest throughout the world seeking to find the dissociated fragments of her psychic other, her lost sense of wholeness, her original self. Eventually Isis succeeds in reassembling Osiris's fragments: ". . . except that his generative member could not be found. So Isis fashioned a new one and impregnated herself by it" (Metzner, 1998, p. 104). Using the language of Western psychology and within the context of this article, Set is a metaphor that characterizes our shadow-self and represents our addiction and the Grammarian worldview.

In referring to this search for our lost half we often tend to believe it means finding a lost physical part of our self that we have become divided from that represents our cosmic twin. This is the personal mythology I once had about finding my lost half. Through my experiences with love, loss, and human relationships, I have continued to revise my thinking about this search for our lost half. I now believe that this search refers to finding that person or persons who, through our interaction with them, assist us in discovering and remembering the unconscious characteristics of our personality that we could not otherwise actualize into our conscious awareness. These are the people who help us become whole, assisting us in remembering the lost constellations of our self. These are the people who help us heal our psychic fragmentation, who assist us in freeing ourselves from our dismembered state of consciousness. These are the people who "know where we are coming from" and with whom our dynamic interchange and dialogue serves to create something new together.

In Search of Our Chosen Relations and a Family–Systems Model of Culture

Finding a book with pages bent and brown
Wandering through the ruins of a city of old
The young man wasn't sure of what he'd found
And so he stopped to read the ancient story it told
Of people in power deep in their ways of war
It was an ageless fire raging out of control
Blinding them to what would be lying before
They never stopped to heed one last desperate call.
Towers of steel in the sunshine glisten
Many will hear but few will listen
Wrapped in their working lives
Unaware that something is wrong.
Signs all around us, nature is warning
Some are protesting, many are scorning
Soon you will realize they cannot come along.

Leave all the lowlands, run to the mountains
Underground springs and natural fountains
Will help you survive the madness you must go through
Move from the cities, run to the country
There will be refuge for only the chosen few.

You who have gazed on this ancient story
Standin' in what's left of our technical glory
You are again from the garden forbidden
In you the seeds of tomorrow are hidden
Prophets and pastors and political masters
Were all swept away when the damage was done
Still from their laughter a choice of disasters
Looms in the distance for those who live on.
(Keith Volquardsen, "Towers of Steel", 1986)

Some of us reading this poem will have negative associations with Volquardsen's reference to "the chosen few", believing it to be an exclusionary statement suggesting that only "God's" chosen people are going to be saved from the collective crises that are threatening the future existence of humankind. This is not how I interpret this statement. I like to think of "the chosen few" as those of us who decide, as a consequence of our own efforts and experiences, to awaken and become part of a group of like-minded seekers who are wandering in search of deeper, more integrated patterns of wholeness. Regarding our search for family, community, and a sense of belongingness, Metzner (1998) provides us with an excellent summary of the archetypal search for our lost half. In his book *The Unfolding Self*, he writes that this search for "the chosen few" has:

> been beautifully expressed in the following paradoxical saying by the great thirteenth-century Chinese Zen Master Ekai, also called Mumon.
>
> > When you understand, you belong to the family;
> > When you do not understand, you are a stranger.
> > Those who do not understand belong to the family,
> > And when they understand they are strangers.
>
> The first line refers to our ordinary situation—accepting conventional social reality and experiencing the acceptance of belonging to a "normal" family. But, as the second line states, one who awakens, who experiences inner realities and questions previous beliefs, will feel like a stranger in the conventional world. The third line tells us that those who seek and question, searching for knowledge and enlightenment, find then that they are part of another family, the family of other alienated seekers, others "who do not understand." They are for him or her what Goethe called the *Wahlverwandschaften*, the "chosen relations." As the fourth line states, these alienated seekers understand only that they are strangers in this world, and because they understand this, they do, in the eyes of the unawakened, become strangers. This is why in so many cultures there are traditions of the "holy fool," the "wise idiot," the eccentric, quirky person who turns out to be the wisest and most enlighten one of all. (p. 253–254)[3]

Nasrudin (in the Sufi stories that I have previously included in this article) is representative of this quirky, yet enlightened person. Likewise as we (the real world counterparts of Nasrudin) experience our own transpersonal awakening—this leads us to begin actively questioning the overriding emphasis on conformity. This awakening alienates us from people whose social–psychological adjustment, enculturation, and cultural amnesia has transformed them into unquestioning members of the herd. In her review of this article, psychologist Zelda Hall reminded me that Tart (1975) referred to this herd mentality as "consensus reality", telling us:

> The prejudice that our ordinary state of consciousness is natural or given is a major obstacle to understanding the nature of mind and states of consciousness. Our perceptions of the world, others, and ourselves, as well as our reactions to (consciousness of) them, are semiarbitrary constructions. Although these constructions must have a minimal match to physical reality to allow survival, most of our lives are spent in *consensus reality*, that specially tailored and selectively perceived segment of reality constructed from the spectrum of human potential. We are simultaneously the beneficiaries and the victims of our culture. Seeing things according to consensus reality is good for holding a culture together, but a major obstacle to personal and scientific understanding of the mind. (p. 33)

Continuing to revise his description of consensus reality, the habits of cognition from which we need to free ourselves, are examples of what Tart (1993) refers to as the psychological defense mechanism *consensus trance*:

> I describe ordinary consciousness as a state-like trance in the pejorative sense of a loss of vitality and initiative, combined with a mechanicalness of thought, feeling and action. The adjective "consensus" is to remind us that the particular form of trance is strongly influenced by the particular culture we are raised in, the implicit and explicit social consensus on what is real and important. (p. 167)

Thus it is not a mandate from some other-worldly God, but our own alienation and aloneness that motivates us to seek out our like-minded "chosen relations" with whom we can begin to create a new sense of community. In an effort toward reconciling our philosophical and transpersonal search for self with our practical concern with family and diversity, I (2009) have pointed out:

> One way to reconcile how to learn from this variety of paradigmatic models is to view their apparent differences as a "Family Systems Model of Culture" or "Systems Model of Ideas and Their Genealogi-

---

[3] Katherine E. Batten (MacDowell) (personal communication, September 29, 2011) pointed out in her review of this article that this search for our "chosen relations":

> is also the underlying meaning of Jesus rejecting his family coupled with always repeating the notions that you will likely be seen as obscure and strange when you arrive to speak/spread the "good news". The enlightenment disrupts the standard social system [as Drengson and Roszak pointed out in referring to technocracy], while providing a new model—the alternation of a family unit within the context of a kind of ecospiritual/integrated framework.

cal Origins." Here I am suggesting that we trace the family histories of different ideological systems back to whomever it was who gave birth to them and their offspring (of course, this is not always easy to do and may not always be possible where domination, [colonization,] or other forces have produced knowledge loss). Then, like understanding one's own genealogical family tree, we can begin to see with whom we are directly related, and who comes from another family. We might then be able to figure out how different ideological families could marry each other and/or at least become friends. In this way we might have a new mode or method of approaching and reconciling the problems of paradigmatic diversity and cultural diversity. This Family Systems approach can also be viewed as a map of ideas and their cultural origins. (p. 54)

Finally, what can we say about Volquardsen's message that we are "again from the garden forbidden?" Is this a cryptic message about humankind's exile from Eden? Most likely it is; however the strange twist Volquardsen adds by saying "in you the seeds of tomorrow are hidden" invites another possibility. One of the most powerful legends of indigenous northern Europe, as Metzner (1994) explains, is the eschatological myth of the Ragnarok, that ". . . is usually translated as the 'twilight of the gods', but more precisely means 'final fate of the gods'" (p. 244). For many of us this evokes the myth of Armageddon where the forces of evil destroy the world, leaving the Earth a barren and uninhabitable place, necessitating a new kingdom of heaven that is sent down to Earth by God. Yet, according to Metzner, this interpretation is not the point the Nordic Ragnarok is trying to teach us; instead he draws our attention to the fact that this final battle does not involve all of the gods. Much to the contrary, it is only the warrior-oriented sky gods that are involved in this cataclysmic Earth transforming battle, which Metzner explains is followed by: "...a renewal of the Earth and a new beginning of life, with a new generation of gods and humans telling stories and remembering ancient knowledge. 'A new green Earth arises...'" (p. 249–250). Consequently the peace-living nature gods and a new generation of humans who were absent from this battle are left to inherit this new green Earth.

Thus the final fate of the gods is a vision of "worldviews in collision," symbolized by the battle between the Logos-oriented male heroes and the forces of nature that they have sought to control. This battle ends with both groups annihilating each other. Today these groups represent technocracy's control of nature and our human-caused climate change. Therefore the grub focused solely on the management and consumption of the immediate material world will need a metamorphosis. In other words, the archetype of the peace loving Silver Surfer within us needs to be actualized. The outcome of this "worldview in metamorphosis" (which is as much a psychological struggle as it is a social, political, and economic clash of cultures) will result in a re-inheritance of the Earth by Eros-oriented butterflies guided by eco-ecstasy, eco-compassion, eco-empathy, cooperation, synthesis, and a co-evolutionary, sustainable orientation with the non-human world.

Epilogue

Like the wandering dervish, those of us who have become concerned about global climate change and many other related eco-crises would like to tell the grammarian that if our strict adherence to the worldview of Euro–American science[4] is more important than the essentials of getting out of the well, then he will have to stay where he is until we have learned to speak properly. However, unlike the story of the grammarian and the dervish, we cannot walk away entirely. This is because the growing numbers of eco-crises are not localized problems that simply impact one person: they affect all of our lives, consequently there is nowhere on Earth that we can go to escape them.

References

Batteau, A. W. (2010). *Technology and culture*. Long Grove, IL: Waveland Press, Inc.

---

[4] Remember this criticism is not a reference to all of science, but science that has been influenced by scientism, technocracy, and cultural amnesia.

Batten (MacDowell), K. E. and Schroll, M. A. (2011). Editors' introduction: Understanding the transpersonal ecosophical perspective. *Restoration Earth:, 1* (1), 5–18.

Capra, F. (1991). *MindWalk*. Hollywood, CA: Triton Pictures.

Devereux, P., Steele, J. & Kubrin, D. (1989). *Earthmind: A modern adventure in ancient wisdom*. New York: Harper & Row.

Drengson, A. (1995). *The practice of technology: Exploring technology, ecophilosophy, and spiritual disciplines for vital links*. Albany, NY: State University of New York Press.

Drengson, A. (2011). Shifting paradigms: From technocrat to planetary person. *Anthropology of Consciousness, 22* (1), 9–32.

Firesign Theater. (1999). *Boom dot bust*. CD Recording. Los Angeles: Rhino Records.

Fromm, E. (1968). *The revolution of hope: Toward a humanized technology*. New York: Harper & Row, Publishers.

Glendinning, C. (1994). *My name is Chellis and I'm in recovery from Western civilization*. Boston: Shambhala.

Huxley, A. (1932/1969). *Brave new world*. New York: Harper & Row.

Kremer, J. W. (1992). The dark night of the scholar: Reflections on culture and ways of knowing. *ReVision, 14* (4), 169–178.

Kremer, J. W. (2000). Millennial twins: An essay into time and place. *ReVision, 22* (3), 29–42.

Kremer, J. W. (2002). Radical presence: Beyond pernicious identity politics and racialism. *ReVision, 24* (3), 11–20.

Masters, T. (1998). Home. *Digital Bitch Shifter*. Lincoln, NE: Guarana Records.

Metzner, R. (1994). *The well of remembrance: Rediscovering the earth wisdom myths of northern Europe*. Boston: Shambhala.

Metzner, R. (1998). *The unfolding self: Varieties of transformative experience*. Novato, CA: Origin Press.

Ornstein, R. E. (1972). *The psychology of consciousness*. New York: The Viking Press.

Orwell, G. (1949). *Nineteen eighty-four*. New York: Harcourt, Brace.

Reps, P. (1998). *Zen flesh, Zen bones: A collection of Zen and pre-Zen writings*. Boston: Tuttle Publishing.

Roszak, T. (1969). *The making of a counter culture: Reflections on the technocratic society and its youthful opposition*. Garden City, NY: Doubleday & Company, Inc.

Roszak, T. (1973). *Where the wasteland ends: Politics and transcendence in postindustrial society*. Garden City, NY: Doubleday & Company, Inc.

Schroll, M. A. (1988). Developments in modern physics and their implications for social and behavioral science. In D. L. Thomas (Ed.), *The religion and family connection: Social science perspectives* (pp. 301–321). Provo, UT: Religious Studies Center/Salt Lake City, Utah: Bookcraft Publishing Co.

Schroll, M. A. (2005). Toward a physical theory of the source of religion. *Anthropology of Consciousness, 16* (1), 56–69.

Schroll, M. A. (2007). Wrestling with Arne Naess: A chronicle of ecopsychology's origins. *The Trumpeter: Journal of Ecosophy, 23* (1), 28–57.

Schroll, M. A. (2009). Language, consciousness and a family systems model of culture. *Anthropology News, 50* (5), 54, 2009.

Schroll, M. A. (2010). Toward a new kind of science and its methods of inquiry. *Anthropology of Consciousness, 21* (1), 1–29.

Schroll, M. A. (2011). Review of Fritjof Capra's film *MindWalk*. *Rhine Online: Psi-News Magazine, 3* (1), 8–11.

Schroll, M. A. (in press). The significance of the Goddess Thealogy journal, the institute for thealogy and deasophy, and their future—Transpersonl ecosophy and religious experience: Philosophical reflections on a typology of healing rituals. *Goddess Thealogy: An Interdisciplinary Journal for the Study of Feminism and Religion, 1* (1).

Schroll, M. A. and Walker, H. (2011). Diagnosing the human superiority complex: Providing evidence the eco-crisis is born of conscious agency. *Anthropology of Consciousness, 22* (1), 39–48.

Shah, I. (1968). The magic horse. *Caravan of dreams*. London: The Octagon Press, pp. 95–104.

Shah, I. (1970). *Tales of the dervishes*. New York: E. P. Dutton & Company, Inc.

Spretnak, C. (1991). *States of grace: The recovery of meaning in the postmodern age*. San Francisco: HarpeSanFrancisco.

Tart, C. T. (1975). *States of consciousness*. New York: E. P. Dutton & Company, Inc.

Tart, C. T. (1993). The structure and dynamics of waking sleep. *Journal of Transpersonal Psychology, 25* (2), 141–168.

Tart, C. T. (2009). What went wrong? The death and rebirth of essential science. *Association for Humanistic Psychology-Perspective*, June/July, 6–7.

Thompson, W. I. (1986). *Pacific shift*. San Francisco: Sierra Club Books.

Thompson, W. I. (1989). *Imaginary landscape: Making worlds of myth and science*. New York: St. Martin's Press.

Volquardsen, K. (1986). Towers of steel. *Watcher*. Lincoln, NE: The Loose, Inc. CD recording.

Watts, A. W. (1970). *Does it matter? Essays on man's relation to materiality*. New York: Vintage Books.

Wood, E. (1957). *Zen dictionary*. New York: Philosophical Library.

Wynne, E. (1987). Storytelling. In S. Foster & M. Little (Eds.), *Betwixt and between: Patterns of masculine and feminine initiation* (pp. 482–488). LaSalle, IL: Open Court.

Zamyatin, Y. (1972). *We* (M. Ginsburg, trans.). New York: Bantam Books.

✢❋✢

MARK A. SCHROLL, Ph.D., Research Adjunct Faculty, Institute of Transpersonal Psychology, Palo Alto, California, and serves on the Advisory Board of *Alternative Therapies in Health and Medicine*. He served as Guest Managing Editor of the special *Anthropology of Consciousness*, 22(1), 2011 issue "From Primordial Anthropology to a Transpersonal Ecosophy", and *Anthropology of Consciousness*, 16(1), 2005 issue "Primordial Visions in an Age of Technology". He co-chaired the 2009 "Bridging Nature and Human Nature" annual Society for the Anthropology of Consciousness conference co-sponsored by the Association for Transpersonal Psychology. He serves on the Editorial Board of *Paranthropology: Journal of Anthropological Approaches to the Paranormal*. He serves on the Windbridge Institute Scientific Advisory Board. He was the Founding Editor of *Rhine Online: Psi-News Magazine*. He Edited *Rhine Online*, 3(1), 2011, the special 2nd-anniversary issue "Sacred Sites, Consciousness, and the Eco-Crisis". He serves on the Editorial Board of *Goddess Thealogy: An International Journal for the Study of Feminism and Religion* and the Board of the Institute for Thealogy and Deasophy. He has been invited to serve as the Co-Editor of the 1st issue of *Goddess Thealogy* with Patricia 'Iolana (In Press). Schroll is a transpersonal cultural theorist and conference organizer with multi-disciplinary interests ranging from philosophy of science to transpersonal ecosophy. Contact: rockphd4@yahoo.com

Tall Tale

Anne Westlund

Westlund, A. (2011). Tall Tale. *Restoration Earth: An Interdisciplinary Journal for the Study of Nature & Civilization, 1*(1), 62. Copyright © The Authors. All rights reserved. For reprint information contact: oceanseminary@verizon.net.

The impossible
a tree growing on the beach
3 feet from the waves

Planted
I can feel the wind
blowing through my boughs

An evergreen
I should fall over
like my neighbor there

The sand I grow in
so poor, so unstable
still, remarkably
I thrive

God whispers in my ear,
"Grow."

My branches reach to the sky
I listen for more instructions,
none come.

The waves batter my trunk
people stare and take my picture.
At night I look at the stars
and Mother Moon.

My roots reach down
to the water table,
Salt air peels bark.

Still, I'm here
something so unbelievable
it must be a lie.

*Biography on page 34

The Tree of Everything:
Acacia Tortilis and the Origins of
the Aesthetic Mind

Jorge Conesa-Sevilla

Conesa-Sevilla, J. (2011). The tree of everything: *Acacia tortilis*. And the origins of the aesthetic mind *Restoration Earth: An Interdisciplinary Journal for the Study of Nature & Civilization, 1*(1), 63–71. Copyright © The Authors. All rights reserved. For reprint information contact: oceanseminary@verizon.net.

Abstract

The wide geographical distribution (and implied *historicity*) of *Acacia tortilis* (a.t.) across the African continent and the Middle East, at a time when our ancestors were dealing with changing environments, makes it a good test case for the idea that this tree is *significant* for survival for sure, but also for the foundations of creative imagination, mythology, artistic innovation, and abstract inspiration. While attempting to provide another explication of what motivates or precipitates "art," we make the safe assumption that distinct groups of humans (some) have used hallucinogenic compounds for a long time, some of the time, producing, accidentally or deliberately, artifacts that may be recognized as having artistry. More importantly, an already big-brained ancestor, *Homo erectus*, with a sophisticated enough mind that is forced to think creatively (out of the old primate box) under the effects of dimethyltryptamine (DMT) and monoamine oxidase (MAO) inhibitors, has acacia tree in his/her mind, stomach, hand, and aesthetic eye: Tree of Life, Tree of Knowledge, *Tree of Everything*.

keywords: *Acacia tortilis*, dimethyltryptamine, monoamine oxidase inhibitor, Paleolithic culture, *Homo erectus*

In gratitude to Maestro Viken Peltekian

In...Hawai'i the "casting off" place of the soul is marked by an old Kukui tree to which the soul must cling, laying hold of a green branch, which has the attributes of the dry, in order to be hurled more quickly with its companions into the "labyrinth that leads to the underworld" lest it lose its way and be left to wander as a stray soul over waste lands of earth.
(Beckwith, 1977, *Hawaiian Mythology*, p. 157)

Introduction

The tree *Acacia tortilis* (a.t.), indigenous to Africa, the Middle East, and now widely distributed around the world into other tropical and sub-tropical areas, is the stereotypical (and in many areas, the ubiquitous) tree of that continent.[1] *Acacia tortilis*[i] is the opening logo and iconic signature of shows such as PBS's *Nature*. Orians (1980) and Ulrich (1979) were the first researchers (ecologists) to suggest that given our evolutionary past, naïve human subjects would show an instinctive or innate preference for the silhouette of acacia trees as part of their *savannah hypothesis* for aesthetic preferences. Specifically, this preference was tested by Balling and Falk (1982) in six age groups (8, 11, 15, 18, 35, and 70+). Eight year olds, the least acculturated of these six groups, showed the strongest preference (statistically significant) for a savannah environment that would include a.t. trees. Their findings suggest an innate, psycho-aesthetic and *biophilic* tendency toward preferring this particular shape and tree (see Figure 1).

According to Orians and Heerwagen (1992), during the Pleistocene (2.6 million years ago [mya] to 12,000 years be-

Figure 1

Acacia tortilis 2003© Frank Dickert, Wikipedia Commons Use.

fore our time [BCE]) when ancestral species such as *Homo erectus* were already thriving in a savannah environment (using fire and sophisticated stone tools), this specific and all-inclusive environment of proto humans living on "a camping trip that lasted a lifetime" and across 2 million years was responsible for shaping, in a deep and fundamental way, some of the natural aesthetic preferences we observe in humans today. It may not be accidental that golf courses and parks tend to be landscaped to resemble these foundational environments. Additionally, and as a practical matter, the widespread distribution of a.t. made it the "go-to grocery store" for resources that would come to produce human culture and consciousness: from ships to toothpicks, from musical instruments to potent mind-altering drugs (Shanon, 2008).

Its wide distribution across the African continent and the Middle East (see Figure 2) at a time when our ancestors were dealing with these changing environments makes it a good test case for the idea that this tree is significant for survival for sure, but also for the foundations of creative imagination, mythology, artistic innovation, and abstract inspiration—our thesis.

Figure 2

Present day distribution of a.t. in Africa and the Middle East
2008 © by Esculapio, Wikipedia Commons Use

Signifying a Tree

Ecosemiotically speaking, a.t., even today, signifies shade, water, a place to hide, a place where animals can be hunted, a place where animals can be scavenged, and a source of nuts and leaves. Its thorny branches and/or sturdy constitution are referenced in most languages associated with cultures in its geographical distribution: Arabic—*samar, sammar, samor, samra, sayyal, seyal, seyyal*; Hebrew—*shitat ha'sochech*; Ndebele—*isanqawe, umsasane, umshishene, umtshatshatsha*; Nyanja—*mzunga, nsangu, nsangunsangu, nyoswa*; Somali—*abak, kura*; Swahili—*mgunga, mugumba, munga*; Tigrigna—*akba, akiba, alla, aqba*; Tswana—*mosu, mosunyana*; and Zulu—*umSasane*.

The Hebrew word for a.t. is *shíttah*, which derives from the Egyptian *shent*, the Coptic *shonte*, and the Arabic *sunt*, all meaning "thorn." Adding to this ecosemiotic relation, a.t. and a similar species, *Acacia seyal*, are referred to as *torrent trees* (*sayl*) because they tend to grow in low-lying areas where water runs or accumulates. Incidentally, a related word in Arabic, *samar*, also used also in reference to both trees, means "evening conversation". (see Bible Concordance Online, 2010a; 2010b)

An indirect but still meaningful connection, the Somali word *abak* comes from the same in Phoenician, where the word *abacus* originates given the ancient custom by mathematicians to use heavy wooden tables made of acacia covered with dust, or *abak*, on which to draw numbers (which could quickly be erased).[2] Incidentally, a table-like and support feature at the top of both Greek Doric and Ionic columns is called also an abacus (Stokstad, 1999). Stokestad refers to it as "table-like" as opposed to "square" or other shape designation (p. 165).

Signifying Gods and Goddesses

The acacia tree itself, or its wood, has had important religious meaning (denotation and connotation). In Egyptian mythology, all the gods are said to have been born under the goddess *Saosis* (Acacia). According to

---

[1] A close second is the African Baobad.

[2] This may be suggestive of why Arabic is written in such a fluid and ornamental fashion, sand being not as restrictive a medium as clay, wax, or papyrus.

the *Egyptian Book of the Dead* (a hieroglyphic found inside a pyramid, fragment #436), the God Horus was born from an acacia tree. Moreover, in another legend, Seth kills Osiris[ii] and puts his body in a coffin (made of acacia?). Seth places the coffin on the River Nile where it floats until it reaches a distant, desert shore. An acacia tree is said to have sprouted around the coffin. Most Egyptian coffins that have been dug out are made of the same wood (Hopson, 2004)

The ancient Egyptians put the acacia to many uses:

> The *Sont* (Arabic), or *Acacia nilotica*, was used for: handles of tools, wooden pegs or nails, clamps, idols, and small boxes or parts of cabinets for which a hard compact wood was required. The seed pods of the *Acacia nilotica* and the bark of the *Acacia sealeh* were both used for tanning skins. Other varieties of Acacia found in the interior or on the confines of the desert were used as the shafts for spears. The Acacia tree also produces a gum, Arabica. (2004)

Figure 3

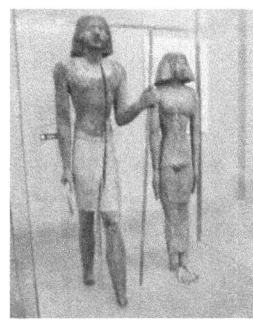

Egyptian, acacia wood, Merti & Wife of Merti, 2380 –2323 BCE; Copyright © 2011 by Joan Ann Lansberry. http://www.joanannlansberry.com /fotoart/met-muzm/merti5d.html

Hopson (2004) further references the acacia as being central to an important biblical story:

> The Bible mentions the acacia (*shittah*) tree a lot since it was exclusively from this wood that the Ark of the Covenant and the Tabernacle were built. This is told in the book of *Exodus*, after Moses received the Ten Commandments on Mount Sinai. The acacia is really the only tree that would have been plentiful in the Sinai Desert. Acacias are commonly found in Israel's and neighboring deserts, often being the only trees in an otherwise empty landscape. For this reason some believe that the Burning Bush spoken of in *Exodus* Chapter 3 was an acacia tree. It was from this Burning Bush that God originally revealed himself to Moses on the slopes of Mount Sinai.

In short, this tree's importance to our ancestors (and related species that share its recognizable silhouette of low hanging branches, easy to climb trunks, and extended shade) cannot be understated. It provided food (roasted pods, sap, and tender shoots), important pharmaceuticals, and the raw materials with which to build an assortment of tools and even musical instruments. Its capacity as a source of widespread building material was specifically related to its aging process into a very hard and red hardwood. It has been further found that in some species, its sap "bleeds" red, secreting a natural insect repellant.[iii]

Even by way of a short introduction, given the ubiquitous historical and geographical presence of acacia trees and their significance to diverse and artistically influential cultures, it is not an exaggeration to call it *the tree of everything*. This claim gains in pre-historical and historical significance when we look, in the next section, at the possible connections between these trees and the development of human consciousness. The phrase "food for thought" may have a more decisive interpretation when it comes to the effects that some substances, extracted from several acacia species, have on human brain chemistry and phenomenology. Just like there is Semitic provenance for having employed a.t. as the raw material for emerging cultures, chemical substances found in the same contain mind-manifesting agents that could have triggered creative and lofty thoughts in *Homo erectus*.

The Tree of Lofty Thoughts

Evolutionary psychologists are, for the most part, shy about studying a possible connection (testable) between the emergence of religion, the nature of religious experience, and the use of hallucinogenic plants. In a relatively recent review of relevant literature, Atran (2002) presents an otherwise interesting set of hypotheses related to the evolution of *mental modules* managing to avoid the topic altogether. Of note, are his proposals that much about the religious experience(s) can be seen as byproducts of two, more general, cognitive modules: *agency* and *classification*. The first would allow *animistic thinking* to become a central feature of religious thinking (something or somebody causes things to happen). The second allows the human mind to taxonomize a complex world into *relevant categories*, ending with the logical conjunction and overlapping with animistic thinking, that these taxonomies are not arbitrary, but are caused.

On the other hand, Dr. Benny Shanon (2008), a psychologist of human consciousness (who happens to be Jewish), has proposed a very interesting (and plausible), and equally controversial theory of consciousness as it relates to Semitic cultures. In a recent article titled *Biblical Entheogens*[3], he introduces a plausible story on the possible mind-manifesting effects of a hallucinogenic substance found in several acacia trees, including a.t. and *Acacia sayal*. The sap and inner bark of both species contain *Dimethyltryptamine* (DMT) [iv], a substance found in other plant species. DMT is one ingredient in *ayahuasca*, the powerful mind-manifesting South American drug, which is extracted from a vine. DMT is also extracted from the seeds of a South American acacia tree, *Anadenanthera peregrina*, to make the snuff inhalant *yopo* used in Venezuela and Brazil. In the same article, Shanon includes a list of almost 100 references, all dealing with the effects of mind-manifesting drugs in several cultures, present and past.

DMT is a chemically unstable component; thus, in order to have its effects, it needs to be combined with a monoamine oxidase inhibitor and compound, or MAO. MAO prevents the deactivation of DMT and thus prolongs its effects.[v] Together, for example, they make up *ayahuasca*—two plant species. In the Middle East, and beyond, the second compound is found in the widely distributed plant *Peganum harmala* or *harmal*. The latter common word, *harmal*, means both "taboo" and "sacred" in Arabic and "taboo" in Hebrew (*herem*). For all these chemicals to work they must be inhaled or smoked. Directly ingesting DMT, for example, does not produce the strongest intoxicant effects. Smoking it or inhaling it is what leads to the hallucinations that produce the mind-manifesting experience.

Shanon's (2008) basic ethnographic observation, independently corroborated, is that:

> In the southern regions of the Holy Land and in the Sinai peninsula there grow two plants containing the molecules that together constitute the key ingredients of one of the most powerful psychedelic substances in existence, the Amazonian brew Ayahuasca. One plant is *Peganum harmala*, harmal in Arabic, the other is Acacia, shita (plural, shittim) in Hebrew; they contain betacarbolines and DMT, respectively. In the Bible, there are no indications of the use of the first plant, but there is clear evidence that the second plant was most valued. From it were made the tabernacle and the ark in which the Mosaic Tablets of the Law were guarded. Nowadays, traditional Arab and Bedouin healers employ both plants in their curative practices…Jews throughout the Middle East use harmal in various forms for medicine and sorcery.

Figure 4

A modern replica of the Ark of the Covenant (unknown illustrator)

His more controversial argument includes many passages he finds, translates, and cites from the Bible (the Jerusalem edition) that describe biblical characters alluding to the use of and/or using these compounds, while describing behavioral and psychological effects consistent with modern interpretations of a drug-induced state. Included in these is a double reference to the effects that the Ark of the Covenant (see Figure 4) could have had on those who were not pure enough to withstand its power–wisdom. Namely, the ark made of *sayl* wood, metaphorically and literally speaking, stands for the possibility of a very bad trip if one's intentions are not honorable. Shanon further writes about the probable extensive ritual use of these two plant species as entheogens by the African-desert Bedouins for a very long time. He cites the observations of Rami Sajdi who hypothesized that Islam and pre-Islamic Arab religions were mystically grounded in the use of entheogens—these two in particular, our desert *soma*.

It may be noted that culture and the particular ecopsychological bonds connecting peoples to places merely modifies the set experience of a hallucinogenic journey. In the cacophonic abundance of the jungle, the trip is animistic and pantheistic. Jaguar and anaconda gods may be only salient characters in a tapestry of

---

[3] An *entheogen* is a mind-manifesting and altering substance used in a religious context.

colors, textures, and voices. In a far away desert, the trip is singular: a monotheistic vision and voice born of solitude or geographical isolation and even alienation. The exuberant flow and waters of the Amazon against an ever-present shouting green generate plurality— both feminine and masculine. The desert mirage is, on the other hand, male and singular.

To start connecting related stories, recall from the introduction that, according to the best evidence, *Homo erectus* is the *homo* species who ventures out of Africa and who invents how to make and control fire. Our own footprints are nearly indistinguishable (see Figures 5 and 6) from theirs. It is not hard to imagine that during the longest period of evolution of our most ancient and direct human line when our ancestors were camping around acacia trees, burning its wood, ingesting its sap (gum Arabica), they might have been the first to experience the mind-altering effects of acacia– DMT. If so, and if these practices continued into the Neolithic pe-

Figure 5

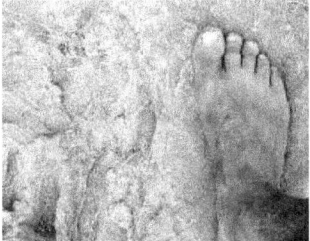

Size and shape comparison of fossilized footprint of Homo erectus (circa 1.5 mya), Africa
Photo: Brian Richmond,
http://www.npr.org/templates/story/
story.php?storyId=101191786

riod, then psycho-aesthetics by any other name is psychedelic-aesthetics long before it was recorded in history. Of course not every hallucinogenic experience will translate into a religious myth or an artifact that gives it credence. Not every hallucinogenic experience will translate into a hyper-glossal storyteller making deep philosophical pronouncements. Not every hallucinogenic experience will translate into a new tool, piece of art, or musical score. Possibly most hallucinogenic experiences do not go beyond a few muted syllables and unintelligible utterances, further disorientation rather than enlightenment. More importantly, an already big-brained ancestor with a sophisticated enough mind, who is forced to think creatively (out of the old primate box) under the effects of DMT and MAO inhibitors, has acacia tree in his/her mind, stomach, hand, and aesthetic eye: Tree of Life, Tree of Knowledge, Tree of Everything.

Figure 6

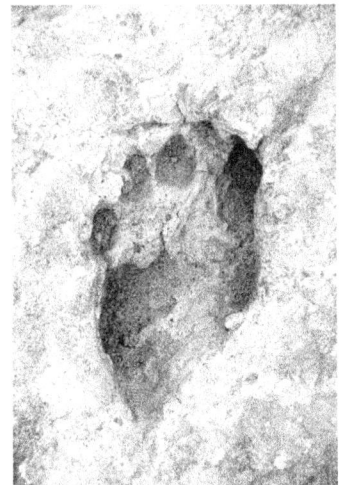

Fossilized footprint of Homo erectus (circa 1.5 mya), Africa.
Photograph: Matthew Bennett
Bournemouth University, at:
http://www.npr.org/templates/story
/story.php?storyId=101191786

Translating Visions into Art

Let us assume that Shanon's (2008) argument and our speculation are both somewhat correct. In its weakest form it assumes that: *distinct groups of humans (some) have used hallucinogenic compounds for a long time. During that time some have produced, accidentally or deliberately, artifacts that can be recognized as having artistry.* This argument is psychologically related to (and also very different from, in some cases) the question: What motivates or precipitates "art" from the head of *Homo erectus*, a being who hunts and gathers in groups, fashions sophisticated biface stone tools, and controls and makes use of fire? What is inside that head, of course, are: anger, love, lust, hunger, fear, kin relations, courage, old age, the feminine, the masculine, what the digging stick does, what the spear kills and that a certain spear point kills more and better, sex, understanding how gravity operates on physical bodies, notions of birth and death (and rebirth), notions of time, notions of time passing, urinating and defecating, color, sounds, smells, saliva, sickness, health, laying prone, standing, standing still, running, making war, making peace, sharing food, hoarding food, water cooling, water flooding, feet, arms, legs, eyes, heads, tongues, a mother's embrace, the expert hands of the elderly, the fire that makes meat so tasty, the fire that roasts the acacia-tree pods and seeds, the smoke of the acacia wood burning, inhaling the same smoke while eating *harmala* for indigestion, staring at the fire under a star-filled savannah sky while listening to a lioness roar…and so much more. There is enough to draw upon, pun intended.

Being generous, there is enough inside *Homo erectus'* head, the first hunter–gatherer *homo* society whom we know of, to begin sentimentalizing about and then wanting to represent a wondrous reality, inner and outer. One can tell that *Homo erectus* was picky about his/her tools. In the Early Paleolithic (1.4 million years to about 100,000 years ago) we find the first biface (Acheulian) flaked tools and the attention to symmetry with the implication that *Homo erectus* understood how this symmetrical tool would translate into a more efficient cutting edge for processing meat (see http://www.originsnet.org/peninjgallery/pages/j)oldef-hrbiffig63.htm for image). More controversial is finding and explaining red ochre, a pigment associated with burial rites, and carved feminine figures in *Homo erectus* sites. If the rest of their material culture were objects made out of fibers and wood, these have not been preserved or found (so far).

However, the intentional knapping of an appropriate mineral or stone into useful shards with specific uses in mind, leaving a symmetrical biface ax, is a giant leap into artistry. It takes a sophisticated aesthetic eye to select a stone of promising characteristics, judge the path of knapping, and sit patiently working on something that could easily cut through a human's hand tendons if distracted. This is the beginning of sculpture, and in the words of Harrod (2002), this process is neither humble nor primitive:

> The knapper, who has made the discovery of, and could now work in, three-dimensional Euclidean space, seems drawn to the novelty of this new power. The knapper emphasizes the sphericity, substantiality, and gravity of this new sense of space and its multiple perspectives and contrasts this with the rising, aspiring, verticality of the column. (p. 5)

Even though stone tools are not usually regarded as "art" artifacts, Harrod (2002) makes the important point that stone tools have an inherent semiotic value in that they represent "invisible components of technology." It would be very hard to agree with Harrod when he proposes an intended male-female symbolism to be read in the lanceolate, biface of Homo erectus tools. A more mundane but equally important semiotic, "invisible component of technology" would be the degree of empathy and craftsmanship identification that, surely, would be elicited in the mindset of a modern knapper (or a marble sculptor for that matter) if they were to reproduce the same artifact without using modern tools!

If today's art is tomorrow's innovation, then the biface already anticipates and is a miniature model of columns, a larger menhir, an obelisk, post-and-lintel construction, the hull of a ship, the encapsulated human form ready to be freed with added negative spaces—a Venus-to-be, polarity, direction, axis, planes, the mass integrity of a certain oval-shaped disk. It is as easy to project forward as it is to project backwards, in hindsight, the rudiments of manufactured geometry. A little puff of acacia–DMT laced with *harmala* could make an artist of the day, even with half a brain, see the future, from *bifaced* to *multifaced*, and even things to come: denuded forests with more advanced versions of Acheulian-on-steroids inventions. Fast forward in time, add more complex culture into the mix, have even brainier *homo* species up to *Sapiens sapiens*, continue the irresistible intake of hallucinogens, and art and technology, traveling like sister and brother along our hominid long journey, will take us almost anywhere.

To reiterate an earlier point, nowhere in this short paper is the argument presented that ingesting mind-manifesting or altering compounds is a necessary requirement to artistic competency. Rather, one can ponder whether at significant junctures in human (artistic, cultural) development, our material culture was so much less that the internal experiences of a DMT–*harmala* trip seemed so much more in comparison—a gift. Otherwise engaged in the harsh realities of surviving savannahs, deserts, and while entering new lands (Europe and Asia), the occasional DMT–*harmala* trip must have made everything pale in comparison—this new reality more terrifying and more beautiful. Thus, in balance, it would also seem incredible to believe that these experiences were devalued or ignored, forgotten, did not contribute, at least once in every generation—in a singular head—to interesting and novel products, including art.

Translating visions into art may occur regardless of where these visions come from: dreams, insights, prayer, or drugs. Shanon (2008) and others have raised the suspicion that others need to test. Namely, that human brains evolved while taking hallucinogens and that their effects were one variable among many other important ones in producing what we now define as "art."

The continuing argument could be that translating visions into art is/has been aided by copious amounts of tea, coffee, alcoholic brewages, Marihuana, and LSD, the preceding, a short list of "uppers", "downers", and mind manifesting drugs, psychochemically assisting, at least, in modulating artistic expression: the high and low muses. Amusing enough, these are parsimonious anecdotes that form the backbone of the best of Art History: troubled and passionate malcontent bohemians who live shorter but inspired lives. They are more: seeking transpersonal experiences beyond the mundane.

Conclusion

Most types of chemical "muses" may have something in common with the most familiar and "original" one, Gaia, worshiped at the oracle at Delphi, Greece, since prehistoric times (de Boer & Hale, 2000). For the ancient Spartan poet Alkman (7th Century BCE), at least, Gaia was one of the original muses (Hutchinson, 2001). Relevant to the many threads presented up to now, the gas *ethylene* has been found to diffuse from rock formations at Delphi and other geologically similar places, trapped in limestone and released by water (de Boer & Hale). Ethylene is both an anesthetic and a euphoriant, thus causal to the observations made since ancient times of supplicants and virginal priestesses falling into inspired trances at this Greek location.

A non-gaseous theory, acacia trees are literally "the tree of life" for so many other animals supporting as they do diverse ecological niche areas and processes. More importantly, they are as ubiquitous as sand and wind in the land of our ancestral origins. From a semiotics of art perspective, one can also add that a.t. is a *semiotically complex coda*. Our ancestors, and present-day bipedal walkers of the African savannah and other open spaces, were/are confronted with semi-arid or grassy expanses that seemed/seem to go on forever into the horizon. Navigating these spaces with a nervous but purposeful bipedal clip obligates visually isolating and remembering where the shady stands of acacia trees grow. Almost as if moving in a point-by-point navigation mode, each tree and stand becomes an interpretable sign post along the way to somewhere. Thus acacia trees are, semiotically speaking, signifiers of important landscape features and ecological dynamics that could save, if they are understood, a hominid's life. Orians (1980) and Ulrich (1979) were among the first to recognize the significance of these various relationships to "mind," and to test our own instinctual response to these shady and thorny trees.

The tree "says" thorn, and blood-colored sap, and tasty pods when roasted, and animals-that-sleep-under-that-we-can-catch. The tree "says" leopards usually haul their kills up its low hanging branches, and sometimes, all we have to do to get that meat is to scare away the big cat with a couple of stones. The tree also says, "Come mothers and give birth, come leaders and make a fire, come children and play, and when you go away, there will likely be another *sayl* tree pointing the way to fresh water."

The tree says, "Eat my flowers, eat the grubs and the birds that eat my flowers, suckle the honey of my sap—chew it, eat the honey made out of my flowers (*mellifera*, the best tasting honey in the world), clean your wounds with my aseptic thorns, eat my tender shoots."

"I am also the tree of knowledge," says *sayl*. *Sayl* says, and it sounds like water running and the easy conversation of confident and unrushed elders, "If you smoke my bark and add another brother plant that grows nearby, you shall know good and evil. If couples stand by my tree trunk, they will understand nakedness, nudity, and the absence of a false ego—you will be terrified and gratified. While under the effects of *sayl* you will dance, you will draw, you will create and recreate each other in my image and each other in your own images. You will identify with leopard, with baboon, with gazelle, with bee, with stone, with rain. And because you already sing and speak with words, you shall pass on our stories to your children. And you shall make images that tell my stories: you shall draw them, you shall carve them, you shall make monuments to all the stories…*art are thou and thou are art*."

Endnotes

i Acacias were first identified by C. Linnaeus in 1773. There are 1,300 species native to six continents. See Book Rags, http://www.bookrags.com/wiki/Acacia.

ii Coincidentally the Egyptian word for scepter, *sekhem*, is associated with power and control given to the pharaohs by Osiris and it may have originated from their word for acacia. This hieroglyph has been interpreted as both a papyrus reed and a wooden paddle made out of acacia wood. A drawing of a sekhem (Wilkinson, 1994, 182–183):

iii The aqueous extract of the fruit, rich in tannin (18–23%), has shown algicidal activity against *Chroccoccus, Closteruim, Coelastrum, Cosmarium, Cyclotella, Euglena, Microcystis, Oscillatoria, Pediastrum, Rivularia, Spirogyra,* and *Spirulina* (Ayoub, as cited in Sajdi, 2010)… Zulu take bark for cough and the Chipi use root for tuberculosis. Masai are intoxicated by the bark and root decoction, which is said to impart courage and aphrodisiac (the root is said to cure impotence). Astringent bark used for diarrhea, dysentery, and leprosy. Bruised leaves are poulticed onto ulcers. According to Hartwell (as cited in Sajdi), the gum or bark is used for cancers and/or tumors (of ear, eye, or testicles) and indurations of liver and spleen, condylomas, and excess flesh.

iv DMT was first synthesized in 1931 and demonstrated to be hallucinogenic in 1956. It has been shown to be present in many plant genera.

v MAO inhibitors are known to have this catalyst effect on other hallucinogens.

References

Atran, S. (2002). *In gods we trust: The evolutionary landscape of religion.* New York: Oxford University Press.

Balling, J.D., & Falk, J.H. (1982). Development of visual preference for natural environments. *Environment and Behavior, 14,* 5–28.

Beckwith, M. (1977). *Hawaiian mythology.* Hawaii: University of Hawaii Press.

de Boer, J.Z., & Hale, J.R. (2000). The geological origins of the oracle at Delphi, Greece. *Geological Society of London, 171,* 399–412.

Harrod, J. B. (2002). Notes on middle Acheulian spirituality: Stone tool logic structure and analogies of the soul. Retrieved September 1, 2010, from http://www.originsnet.org/machultool1183k.pdf.

Bible Concordance Online. (2010a). Hebrew Dictionary. Retrieved September 1, 2010, from http://strongsnumbers.com/hebrew/5569.htm

Bible Concordance Online. (2010b). Indo-European Dictionary. Retrieved September 1, 2010, from http://strongsnumbers.com/hebrew/5569.htm

Hopson, A. (2004). Acacia. *Encyclopedia Mythica.* Retrieved September 1, 2010, from http://www.pantheon.org/articles/a/acacia.html. (Original publication 1998).

Hutchinson, G. (2001). *Greek lyric poetry: A commentary on selected larger pieces.* New York: Oxford University Press.

Orians, G. (1980). Habitat selection: General theory and applications to human behavior. In J. Lockard (Ed.), *The evolution of human social behavior* (pp.49–66). Chicago: Elsevier.

Orians, G., & Heerwagen, J. (1992). Evolved responses to landscapes. In J. Barkow, L. Cosmides, & J.

Tooby (Eds.), *The adapted mind: Evolutionary psychology and the generation of culture* (pp. 555–579). New York: Oxford University Press.

Sajdi, R. (2010). Desert Land. Retrieved September 1, 2010, from http://www.acacialand.com/ShamnicPlants.html

Shannon, B. (2008). Biblical entheogens: A speculative hypothesis. *Time and Mind: The Journal of Archaeology, Consciousness, and Culture, 1*(1), 51–74.

Stokestad, M. (1999). *Art history* (Rev. ed., Vol. 1). New York: Prentice Hall, Inc. and Harry N. Abrams Inc.

Ulrich, R. (1979). Visual landscapes and psychological well-being. *Landscape Research, 4*(1), 17–23.

Wilkinson, R. H. (1994). *Reading Egyptian art*. London: Thames & Hudson. pp. 182–183; graphic used with permission.

JORGE CONESA-SEVILLA, Ph.D., was born in Caracas, Venezuela, of Catalan parents and has lived in the United States since 1975. He has a BA from Humboldt State University (1989; Bio-Phil-Psy) and a B.A. from Northland College (2010; Fine Arts/Studio). Additionally, he pursued graduate degrees at the University of Toledo, OH (MA: 1992, PhD: 1996; Neurocognition). He has conducted original research on and published about Isolated Sleep Paralysis and Lucid Dreaming. A student of the late Bill Devall, Jorge approaches "green psychology" from diverse perspectives: Human Ecology, Integral Ecology, Evolutionary Science, Eco- & Biosemiotics, General Semantics, and Deep Ecology. He is particularly interested in the fusion of Paul Shepard's work, "ecopsychology," and Evolutionary Psychology: Evolutionary Ecopsychology. Now living in Maui, he leads Psychology in The Wilderness courses.
Website: http://www.wix.com/jorgeconesasevilla/ecopsychology

"A Tree's Perspective" copyright © 2009 by Katherine Batten MacDowell. Photo taken in New Jersey, USA.

Altering Consciousness: Ayahuasca & the Shamanic Path to Wholeness

Simon Ralli Robinson

Robinson, S.R. (2011). Altering consciousness: Ayahuasca & the shamanic path to wholeness. *Restoration Earth: An Interdisciplinary Journal for the Study of Nature & Civilization, 1*(1), 72–77.

Abstract

Ayahuasca is a mystical brew, known to have been drunk for millennia by shamans in the Amazon basin in order to gain access to extraordinary altered states of consciousness in which they claim they are able to commune with the spirits of plants, gaining "true" medical knowledge of their healing properties and giving the curanderos the ability to "see" the illness in patients. Ayahuasca as a hallucinogen only began to come to the awareness of westerners in the last 30 years, and as such there is a dearth of scientific evaluation and study of both the drink and the modality of healing with which it is used. This paper describes the range of experiences that have been classified by psychologist Benny Shanon, and adds to these by describing my own experiences as an apprentice ayahuasca curandero, the process by which a student is initiated into the healing secrets of the sacred medicine.

Introduction

It is now more than 30 years since Fritjof Capra wrote *The Tao of Physics* (1975) highlighting the remarkable similarities between Eastern religions and Western quantum physics. These insights, as Capra openly revealed in the preface, were inspired by his own personal experiences with what he called "power plants" (p. 12): plants that have been ingested by shamans for a millennia and revered by peoples across the world as divine beings. The hallucinogenic properties of these power plants resulted in such extraordinary changes to human consciousness for the shaman that it cannot be distinguished from the spiritual and religious revelations seen in mystics and sages down through the centuries; indeed scholars have speculated that the foundation of Western mystical traditions have their origins in the use of power plants (see Ruck, Staples, Celdrán, & Hoffman, 2007).

Capra was by no means the first scientist to gain deeper insights into the natural world from natural and synthetic hallucinogens. Alan Rees (2004), writing in The Mail on Sunday, revealed the following story, which he subsequently confirmed with Francis Crick, in person:

> Dick Kemp told me he met Francis Crick at Cambridge. Crick had told him that some Cambridge academics used LSD[1] in tiny amounts as a thinking tool, to liberate them from preconceptions and let their genius wander freely to new ideas. Crick told him he had perceived the double-helix shape while on LSD.[2]

The classic psychedelics are considered to be LSD, Psilocybin, DMT[3], and mescaline. The two chemical groups into which these drugs are classified are the tryptamines and the phenethylamines. Tryptamines include DMT, psilocybin, LSD and Tabernanthe iboga. Phenethylamines include mescaline found in the peyote cactus and the lesser-known San Pedro cactus (Robinson, 2011, p. 92). I have been told by shaman from the Amazon that Ayahuasca is generally considered to be the world's strongest hallucinogens (with perhaps only the plant toé being stronger but of little use as a workable hallucinogen due to the high possibly of death when ingesting it). It is Ayahuasca that I shall now explore in detail.

[1] Lysergic acid diethylamide

[2] "Nobel Prize genius Crick was high on LSD when he discovered the secret of life" (Rees, 2004)

[3] Dimethyltryptamine

The Plant Power of the Amazon Basin: Ayahuasca

In the Amazon basin, indigenous and mestizo shamans drink the mystical and sacred brew Ayahuasca, a drink made from the vine Banisteriopsis caapi (Bc) and leaves from either the Psychotria viridis (Pv) or Diplopterys cabrerana (Dc). Locally these shamans refer to the vine by many different names, such as: yagé, caapi, vine of the souls, vine of the dead, or ayahuasca. This vine contains three monoamine oxidase inhibitors—harmine, harmaline, and tetrahydroharmine—that are hallucinogenic at sufficient dose levels and is referred to as the base of the drink. Shamans then add to the drink leaves of the chacruna plant (Pv) or the huambisa plant (Dc), which are viewed as the "light" or the source of hallucinations. The leaves of each of these plants contain DMT that is also present in the human brain. However, the hallucinogens are not active orally since it is blocked by monoamine oxidase (a stomach enzyme) and thus Bc is required as it inhibits this stomach enzyme, enabling the DMT enter the brain. While Bc and Pc are the typical ingredients of the drink, different shamans may add or adjust the ingredients according to the needed magical or healing outcomes (for example: cleansing, spiritual protection, enhancement of visions, and physical healing). Examples of additional plants utilized are the *toé* (*Brugmansia suaveolens*), tobacco, pirri pirri (*Cyperus* spp.), marosa (*Irisene* sp.) (Robinson, 2011, p. 162).

While illegal in many countries due to the active ingredient DMT being a class A category drug, ayahuasca remains legal in Peru and Brazil where a number of syncretic churches incorporate ayahuasca into their Christian and mystical services. Thousands of "ayahuasca tourists" fly to Peru each year to take part in ceremonies, and it is increasingly becoming available in North America, Europe, and Australia, although those who do drink it rarely do so for purely recreational use due to the risks involved. The side effects of ayahuasca can include severe vomiting and diarrhea. Further the visions brought about by ingestion can provoke utter terror in those who experience them and who are unprepared for them. Further making this drink rarely utilized for recreational purposes is the degree of physical preparation necessary to produce the hallucinatory effects: the drinker must undertake a period of detoxification and abstinence from many different foods (including coffee, alcohol, red meat, sugar, spices and salt), making this drink almost impossible for people to abuse. Additionally, ayahuasca is far more likely to provide some of the harshest lessons in life to those who attempt to use it, particularly when used without guidance and preparation (Robinson, 2011).

The Psychological Experience of Ayahuasca Through a Western Lens

Until around 1990, the main scientific interest in ayahuasca was in botany, chemistry, human neuropharmacology, and anthropology. It was at this time that psychology began to explore the effects of ayahuasca on consciousness and cognition. One of the key figures in this research is Benny Shanon (2002), a cognitive psychologist who first attempted to chart the phenomenological ayahuasca experience from a psychological perspective. Ten years of research contributed to the most comprehensive psychological study of ayahuasca ever undertaken, with over 2,500 user reports analyzed. These were complemented by Shanon's own personal participation in about 130 ceremonies, a huge number for a scientist to have taken part in. Shanon asked, "What is experienced when one drinks ayahuasca?" and he answered this question by looking at the experience from many different perspectives:
- Structural typology
- Style of visual images
- Interaction and narration
- The contents of visions
- The themes of visions
- Ideas, insights and reflections
- Alterations to consciousness and perception of time

- Non-visual perceptions
- Stages and progression of visions within and across ceremonies

More recently, Shanon (2010) has expanded his topological framework to examine in more detail the deep epistemological questions of meaning and interpretation of those who experience ayahuasca at its most ineffable and transcendental levels, and for whom orthodox theories of psychology become woefully inadequate. This observation comes from the many ceremonies I took part in between 2008 and 2010, with shamans who had themselves spent anywhere between two and ten years alone in the deep virgin rainforest, experiencing communion and lessons from the spirits of plants in a mode of consciousness that from personal experience is far beyond that which any form of words, logic or symbols are able to adequately convey. Shanon provides these high level categories within which drinkers of *ayahuasca* place their experiences:

Psychological Knowledge
Ayahuasca can provide novel insights and self-understanding. One or two ayahuasca sessions are often described as being the equivalent of years of psychoanalysis.

Knowledge Related to Nature and Life
Ayahuasca drinkers will often experience a profoundly close link to nature, animals, plants, and minerals, especially when it is drunk in the natural setting of the Amazonian rainforest. These experiences can be extraordinary for those who have them. For example, they might transform into an eagle flying above the rainforest canopy or really experience what it is like to be a certain animal, plant, or tree.

Philosophy and Metaphysics
Ayahuasca can generate philosophical and metaphysical ideations and reflections. In 2009 during my first year's apprenticeship I received deeply intuitive understandings of the symbolism of the ankh, Thoth, David Bohm's implicate order framework of quantum physics, and the Tao. These experiences utterly defy any attempts to be captured in words, reflecting the teachings from many Eastern religions that true reality is beyond language, words, and human understanding.

Artistic Performance and Creativity
When under the influence of ayahuasca, the level of musical, singing, and occasionally dancing performances is greatly enhanced. I have found that when singing icaros, sacred healing songs of which I have been taught, I have sung with a delicacy, intonation, and vibrato that I could never think of achieving outside of an *ayahuasca* ceremony. I had one experience in 2010 when I was working on a patient with deep emotional issues, and I feel that the singing almost entirely came from my heart, as I healed her dark emotional pains. For me to reach this level of singing, I first had to undertake many grueling ceremonies, clearing out my own blocks and emotional pain. This was a journey from head to heart consciousness, and I now feel that I can live each day far lighter, more open, and in tune with our natural world.

Specialized and Factual Knowledge
Shanon (2010) emphatically explains that he does not believe in paranormal or parapsychological phenomena, and he is explicit in stating that he has found no instance in which an individual has obtained new factual evidence through drinking ayahuasca. This is in direct contrast to Stanislav Grof (2009), who provides compelling evidence that this is the case with those who are administered LSD in a supportive psychotherapeutic context, suggesting that it is equally plausible that a DMT-based substance could provide similar benefits.

Only a very tiny proportion of Shanon's research (2002, 2010) has been with indigenous or Mestizo shamans, who for centuries (or more likely millennia) have drunk ayahuasca in order to diagnose illness "supernaturally". They do so in partnership with the spirits of the plants, who they refer to as *los doctores*. Shanon collated personal reports of the phenomena, but did not complement these with any other forms of analysis or experimentation. Shanon's interpretation is that *ayahuasca* provides a heightened state of awareness that taps into preexisting states of empirical knowledge and practice.

The Mestizo Way of Ayahuasca

The shamanic healers in the Amazon who drink ayahuasca to diagnose illness are more commonly known as curanderos, and their training and experience with ayahuasca generally starts when they are in their teens. They will, from an early age, be taught by their maestro (teacher), to recognize thousands of plants and their healing properties. However, to really get to know ayahuasca and the spirits of the plants, the apprentice curandero has to spend not months but years alone in the rainforest with no clothes and only a blanket. They must follow an extremely limited diet of mainly fish, plantain, and other jungle fruit. In these years of solitude, the apprentice will drink both ayahuasca and samples of every plant, flower, or tree that they will be using as future medicines in order to become intimate with the properties and spirits of those plants.

After the years of apprenticeship are over, the apprentice returns as a curandero, capable of healing in partnership with the spirits of the plants they formed a relationship with while in the wilderness. The shaman heals holistically by determining what "illness" is trapped within the patient's soul or spiritual body. This form of illness is conceived as an energy imbalance, where emotions and negative thinking may become trapped in the physical body causing pain, dysfunction, or disease. In order to heal a patient, the plants will show the shaman where these concentrations of negative energy are in the spiritual body. The shaman will then use a combination of techniques to extract these negative energies. These include the singing of sacred songs (icaros) while playing shacapa (an instrument made from dried leaves of the carrizo plant), blowing tobacco smoke, blowing sacred breath into the spiritual body (soplas), and also sucking the energy out of the body (chupas) (Robinson, 2011). What marks Amazonian healers out as different to most other healing modalities, including shamanic healing in other countries, is the shaman's use of the hallucinogenic drink *ayahuasca* with which they use to learn from the spirits of plants, and with which they drink to analyze and heal patients. Although highly controversial, having undertaken an apprenticeship with my own *Maestro curandero*, I do feel that this mode of healing deserves much greater analysis and understanding from the western medical communities, and it is this mode of healing I will describe now in more detail.

Healing Through Ayahuasca: My Apprenticeship

Following a sudden growth of interest with Westerners in the last 20 years, a number of books about ayahuasca have been published, but very few have documented in any detail the incredibly rich and sophisticated pharmacological knowledge and conceptual frameworks of illness developed by the curanderos (Luna, 1984; Beyer, 2009). There have been no medical studies of this healing modality, despite much anecdotal evidence of its efficacy and shamanism's position as the oldest spiritual and healing practice in the world. However, the relatively new multidisciplinary field of ethnopharmacology is starting to redress this issue.

The approach I have taken with my ayahuasca research has been to complement both the works of Shanon (2002, 2010) and Beyer (2009) with a comprehensive and structured phenomenological account of my own experiences as an apprentice ayahuasca curandero (Robinson, 2010). I first travelled to Peru in 2008 to participate in a two week ayahuasca retreat in order to heal some deep psychological traumas from my past. I then decided to return to Peru in 2009, simply to participate in some further ayahuasca ceremonies with Javier Arevalo, but to my surprise, and without asking, I was taken on as his apprentice.

Javier continually emphasized to me that the visions experienced by both an apprentice and maestro shaman are qualitatively different to those of participants or patients. Javier initiated me into the secrets of the shacapa, taught me icaros, and how to perform the sopla (the sacred healing breath on a patient).

Within any literature on curanderos, it is extremely rare to read an account by a Westerner who has been taught how to perform a diagnosis via conscious communication with the spirits of plants, using the full range of shamanic techniques, as I have attempt to do so here.

The first thing I had to learn is how to move from head consciousness to heart consciousness. I learned to really trust ayahuasca rather than fight it, and this lesson was probably the hardest. It involved a shamanic initiation by the ayahuasca itself whereby my body was slowly killed off, one vital organ at a time. This was not a visual hallucination. I believed that what I was experiencing was real. It was terrifying to the point that a trained therapist told me it was the worst psychotic episode she had ever witnessed. Many people do not go back to ayahuasca having experienced the legendary terrors that it can bring, but I did.

Javier structured my lessons so that initially I would drink a mild ayahuasca. I was slowly introduced to *los doctores*—or perhaps they slowly introduced themselves—and they showed me how to diagnose illness, not through any form of empirical language-based knowledge, but in a more visual, direct, and intuitive way. It is this form of curandero knowledge to which Shanon makes no reference. This might reflect his lack of this specific ayahuasca experience. In each ceremony the doctores taught me by showing how they were healing my own body. It was an experience that I would learn has rarely been described in ayahuasca literature.

Although it is nigh on impossible to explain what is an ineffable experience I will try. Ayahuasca can be said to make your body transparent, and I certainly found this to be the case. I was lying down in the darkness of a temple in the rainforest listening to Javier's beautiful icaros calling the doctores to us. Around an hour after first ingesting the brew, I sensed them approaching. I often experienced them, not as Beyer's (2009) human forms, but as fantastic matrices of light, highly organic structures that danced as they flew, fusing with my own consciousness so that we would become one. My physical body gradually began to melt into nothingness, and I experienced a vast expansion of my own consciousness that corresponded with seeing the doctores expand into many dimensions. Their canopies of light would unfold in such a way that if was like being in a hyper-dimensional, brilliantly electroluminescent cathedral looking up at an ever expanding ceiling of beams, arches, and patterns stretching into an impossible vastness that was mine, or our, expanded consciousness.

Then the doctors "flew" to any particular part of my body requiring treatment and showed me symbolically where the negative energy was. Of course, this energy had to be expelled, and this is done via the purge (vomiting, diarrhea, or both). When working with a patient, the doctores are able to be extremely precise in locating the area of the body in which the illness resides. In one patient, a very young child, I was shown dark menacing insects in his urinary system and was shown the achiote plant that was to be used as the cure. After the ceremony, Javier confirmed that the child did indeed have an infection in this area and that the achiote was the correct plant for the cure.

Are the visions of the shaman qualitatively different from participants or patients? A curandero will drink ayahuasca thousands of times, unlike the vast majority of Westerners who travel to Peru and the wider Amazon to take part in perhaps only one, two, or a very small handful of ceremonies. These initial ceremonies can be spectacular (for example, the reports of metamorphosing into eagles flying over the canopy of the rainforest), but Javier was clear that these experiences provide only a very cursory insight into the spiritual world. What I experienced was initially disorientating, going far beyond any form of words, going far beyond any kind of world that had the structure of three dimensions and time. It was a world that could only be experienced with a parallel and extreme alteration and expansion to my consciousness.

Time and again, those who have ingested ayahuasca and other hallucinogens report that they experience reality as an undivided wholeness and also that both time and space cease to exist. It is intriguing to speculate that perhaps one of the effects of hallucinogens in the brain is to enable the person to experience the implicate order of David Bohm (1980) directly. Bohm's concept of wholeness and the implicate order certainly can be seen as very shamanic in nature (and can also be likened to the metaphysics of, for example, Taoism or Hinduism). Javier continually emphasized that this world is an illusion and that only the spiritual world mattered or is the true reality. I asked for clarification, in terms of the relationship of this world to the spiritual world, and rather than giving a Platonic or dualist account, Javier said that although the material world was a part of the spiritual world, it was just one tiny fragment, mirroring the way in which Bohm describes the relationship of the explicate to the implicate.

The concept of expansion came up many times in ceremonies. In one particular ceremony, Ayahuasca told me that science could only advance if it made the transition from reduction to expansion. I feel that it is now time to expand our thinking away from a reliance on reductionism to include the very ancient concepts of wholeness. This wholeness can really only be experienced in an intuitive mode of consciousness, which natural plant hallucinogens facilitate if they are treated with the reverence and respect. Further by opening up to the ways of knowing that remain embedded in many indigenous cultures across the planet, we may find guides on our journeys to wholeness and open up a vast new expanse of knowledge that is holistic in every sense of the word.

References

Beyer, S.V. (2009) *Singing to the plants A guide to Mestizo Shamanism in the Upper Amazon.* Albuquerque: University of New Mexico Press

Bohm, D. (1980). *Wholeness and the implicate order.* London: Routledge.

Capra, F. (1975). *The Tao of physics.* Boston: Shambhala.

Grof, S. (2009). *LSD: Doorway to the numinous.* Rochester: Park Street Press. (Original publication as *Realms of the Human Unconscious*, 1975).

Luna, L.E. (1984). The concept of plants as teachers among four Mestizo shaman of Iquitos, Northeastern Perú. *Journal of Ethnopharmacology, 11,* 135–156.

Rees, A. (2004, September 4). Nobel Prize genius Crick was high on LSD when he discovered the secret of life The Mail on Sunday

Robinson, S.R. (2011). *The shaman and Snow White: Ayahuasca, San Pedro, shamanic states of consicousness and certificate 18 healing.* Dumfries, Lulu.

Ruck, C.A.P., Staples, B.D., Celdrán, J.A.G., & Hoffman, M.A. (2007). *The hidden world: Survival of pagan shamanic themes in European fairytales.* Durham, North Carolina: Carolina Academic Press.

Shanon, B. (2002). *The Antipodes of the mind: charting the phenomenology of the ayahuasca experience.* Oxford: Oxford University Press.

Shanon, B. (2010). The Epistemics of ayahuasca visions. Phenomenology of Cognitive Science, 9(2), 263–280.

Note: An earlier version of this article was published in *Holistic Science Journal* under the title "Altered states of consciousness and the shamanic path to wholeness—Healing with natural plant hallucinogens and the spirits of nature"

SIMON RALLI ROBINSON is the author of the book *The Shaman and Snow White: Ayahuasca, San Pedro, Shamanic States of Consciousness and Certificate 18 Healing.* He has a master's degree in Holistic Science from Schumacher College and Plymouth University and is the editor of the blogs www.transitionconsciousness.org and www.shamanicdrumming.co.uk.

The Next Layer

Anne Westlund

Westlund, A. (2011). The next layer. *Restoration Earth: An Inter-disciplinary Journal for the Study of Nature & Civilization*, *1*(1), 78.
Copyright © The Authors. All rights reserved. For reprint information contact: oceanseminary@verizon.net.

Digging
not too deep
just enough to be painful
below the surface

what was man-made
is still visible
on top of everything
like my red-dyed hair
like the clothes on my body.

A few inches below
things are darker, finer
the weeds of civilization
take root here.

He wants more from me
I know
than what's on the surface
what everyone can see.

Sometimes it's so difficult
to turn away from the glare
that sudden flash
my shape (round) forever on film
the light of the Marketplace

and get down to the real me
what I believe, who I am
goes unrevealed, unnoticed.

Still
God sees the truth
helps me—
to uncover my honesty.

this is Love.

*Biography on page 34

Vision Quest—Awakening Transpersonal Ecopsophy: Practical Solutions Toward a Sustainable Culture

Mark A. Schroll

Schroll, M.A. (2011). Vision quest—awakening transpersonal ecopsophy: Practical solutions toward a sustainable culture.. *Restoration Earth: An Interdisciplinary Journal for the Study of Nature & Civilization, 1*(1), 79–83. Copyright © The Authors. All rights reserved. For reprint information contact: oceanseminary@verizon.net.

To those unfamiliar with transpersonal ecosophy, it sounds very esoteric and disengaged from practical social concerns and economic reality. In this article I point out that without the internal psychological wisdom of transpersonal ecosophy to guide us, our social actions and economic concerns operate without a personal value system. But how does this process actually take place and how does it lead to practical solutions toward solving the eco-crisis? I offer my own awakening of transpersonal ecosophy as a means of answering these questions.

What Is Transpersonal Ecosophy?

As Guest Managing Editor of *Anthropology of Consciousness*, *22* (1), 2011, I stated clearly in its introduction that at the 2009 Society for the Anthropology of Consciousness forum "The History and Future of Ecopsychology":

> Alan Drengson pointed out that in response to Warwick Fox's *Toward a Transpersonal Ecology* (1990) that Arne Naess said a better title would have been "Toward a Transpersonal Ecosophy." This is because Naess' view of self-realization embodies a transpersonal perspective that derives from his personal philosophical approach that he called Ecosophy-T. Ecosophy, meaning "a philosophy of ecological harmony or equilibrium. A philosophy as a kind of sofia (or wisdom . . . The T refers to his mountain hut Tvergastein" (Drengson and Devall 2008:6-7). "The Deep Ecology Movement" (private distribution). "Ecosophy is [a] creation of relationships which honor all others as subjects, whether these are humans, animals, plants, or inanimate beings" (Drengson 1991:2). "Process, Relationships and Ecosophy" (private distribution). Transpersonal ecosophy also embodies experiential insight derived from techniques of consciousness expansion that liberate us from the "human superiority complex. . ." (Metzner 1999) . . . Transpersonal ecosophy represents liberation from the paradigmatic restrictions that . . . perceive any state of consciousness that is not within the normal range of consciousness as abnormal (Tart 1975) [Schroll 2009:8-9].(Schroll, 2011, p. 4)

Hopefully this definition of transpersonal ecosophy offers all of us inspiring words to live by. Still this definition leaves us asking the practical question how is it useful toward solving any or all problems associated with the eco-crisis? Let us begin by understanding how the perspective of transpersonal ecosophy was awakened in my own way of being.

An Unintended Vision Quest:
Kentucky Wilderness and Transpersonal Ecosophy

In terms of any traditional meaning or intention of what embarking on a vision quest implies (Metzner, 1999), this had nothing to do with this example that begins on June 21, 1980, the summer solstice. Nevertheless (although I was unaware of it at the time), the events that motivated me to embark on this journey do represent those associated with traditional vision quests. The seeds of this story were planted in late April 1980 when I chose to take a break from my studies and visit a local nightclub where live bands performed in Kearney, Nebraska. Hours later upon leaving the nightclub to return home, I witnessed two local Kearney residents hassling a homeless hitchhiker. I intervened on behalf of the hitchhiker, defending the man's right to sit outside the nightclub. Following this incident I invited the hitchhiker to my apartment where I had an extra guest room that I offered to him as a place to spend the night.

That evening he told me the story about thousands of homeless men and women from across the USA who were able to survive off the surplus of what people would throw away. He called these survivalists "Rainbow Warriors". He went on to tell me that each year these Rainbow Warriors had a gathering of the "tribes" for a week or two at the Rainbow Family Gathering to exchange love, support, and acknowledge the passing of another year in our troubled world. He added that the 1980 gathering was to be held the last week in June in the Appalachian Mountains between West Virginia and Virginia.

I responded to his story by saying that I agreed our world was indeed a troubled place and that I was studying psychology, sociology, philosophy, and education to learn how to help build a better world. His reply was that book learning could teach a person how to think, reason, and develop theoretical models (all of which are helpful in understanding the overall picture of any particular problem); however if I was sincerely serious about wanting to make the world a better place then attending the Rainbow Family Gathering was a good place to start meeting others who were already putting their ideas toward improving our world into practice. Finally, he expressed a special concern about the growing eco-crisis that he said was becoming a serious health threat to the quality of life on our planet. Then in the morning I bid him farewell.

I decided to take the homeless hitchhiker's advice to attend the Rainbow Family Gathering that June. Since I had never hitchhiked before, I arranged to get a ride as far as Columbus, Ohio, with my cousin, who was driving to upstate New York to attend summer-school classes at Alfred University. This then is where my journey began.

I began hitchhiking in Columbus, Ohio, and by early evening I arrived at a truck stop on the outskirts of Lexington, Kentucky. Awaiting my next ride I began a conversation with two young men near my age that convinced me to visit Natural Bridge Park, just a few miles from the truck stop. Without any apprehension (a consequence of my naïve trust at the age of 22), I agreed to allow these two strangers to drop me off in pitch darkness where I rolled out my sleeping bag and lay down to sleep that first night on the road in Daniel Boon National Forest.

Upon waking I began hiking; during the first two days I enjoyed taking baths in the cool mountain streams and experiencing the solitude of the wilderness. But by the fourth day I realized I was getting hopelessly lost and chose to find my way back. Four days later I reached the campground where I began—a stark contrast to the wilderness I had been living in during the last eight days. I noticed the walkways, campground, and nearby caves were littered with garbage, such as bottles, cans, paper, etc.... Spending the night in the campground I awoke smelling rotting garbage; something I had not noticed eight days ago deep in the woods.

I can only attribute noticing this smell to living in wilderness for eight days. Smelling these noxious vapors and seeing garbage strewn throughout the surrounding campground motivated me to want to clean up this park. I spent the rest of the day looking for a ranger station where I could present this proposal. Finding a park ranger by late afternoon, I explained my concerns and willingness to volunteer to clean up the horrible mess ruining Natural Bridge Park. He responded by asking, "where's your park pass, son?" Bewildered by this question and this ranger's lack of enthusiasm regarding my willingness help, I said, "I didn't know I needed one." I quickly added that whatever the cost of the pass I was eager to volunteer my services to the state of Kentucky instead of paying the camping fee. The ranger replied he did not need any "long-haired Yankee helping him do [his] job." These eight days in the wilderness, the sudden recognition of the degree to which a natural landscape had been polluted by campers, and the confrontation with the Ranger's unwillingness to allow me to help clean up all formed the foundation of my unorthodox and totally unplanned vision quest that would come to fundamentally awaken my transpersonal ecosophy. The sum total of these experiences from the random hitchhiker I met to my final departure from the woods would shape my transpersonal–ecosophical perspective and ground it in a practical orientation of social and economic concern and change. (Needless to say, for those wondering if I ever made it to the Rainbow Family Gathering, I recognized quickly that I was ill-equipped to hike through the forest and so ended my journey to attend.)

State Funds Wasted on KSC Recycling Program

In August, 1980, back in Nebraska, I returned to Kearney State College (KSC) still thinking about my experience in Kentucky and it occurred to me that there was an untapped strategy that would benefit students and the environment alike right there on the college campus. The idea that I began talking to students, faculty, and school administrators about was the possibility of creating a scholarship based on recycling aluminum cans. I pointed out that throwing away aluminum cans was equivalent to throwing money away; yet none of the students, faculty, or administrators with whom I discussed this idea were interested in getting involved. I did, nevertheless, convince several custodians and grounds–maintenance crews to begin recycling aluminum cans. Ten more years would pass before the rest of this story would begin to unfold.

In honor of the 20th anniversary of Earth Day a groundswell of environmental interest was generated by a barrage of media promoted in the fall of 1989 by various celebrities. In Nebraska this resurgence of environmental concern formed itself into the student organization Ecology Now. One of Ecology Now's first priorities (that I learned by attending its meetings) was to implement an aluminum recycling program on campus. Hearing this I told Ecology Now's members about my 1980's efforts to fund a scholarship with money from aluminum cans, how this was rejected, and how later I had convinced some custodians and grounds–maintenance crews to recycle cans for the past ten years. In response several members of Ecology Now became curious and began inquiring into my efforts and this inquiry produced unexpected consequences.

Concurrent during this same time were efforts by the KSC administration to merge it with the university system in Nebraska. Its petition for acceptance required not only the demonstration of the scholastic excellence of the school's curriculum, but also the demonstration that KSC meet the fiscal requirements. Specifically KSC had to demonstrate that its annual revenues would be a financial asset and not a burden on the university system.

Meanwhile through Ecology Now's inquiry into the recycling of aluminum cans on campus, the KSC administration found out about this recycling activity. Somewhere in the process of investigating this recycling activity the amount of money it generated was considerably inflated. Thus the school administrators saw this as a golden opportunity to enhance their fiscal reserves. In February 1990 the KSC physical plant implemented an aluminum can recycling program in conjunction with its treasury collection procedures at the Foundation Office.

Due to my previous interest in these recycling efforts, I spent ten months investigating this program. I concluded it was unsound because: a) it was only 30% effective in recycling the total amount of aluminum cans because the morale of the physical plant employees and KSC custodial staff was low; and b) employee morale was low because they were never asked to join a recycling effort, but rather were ordered by a mandate that if aluminum can recycling was not carried out for the State of Nebraska, the employee could be reprimanded and possibly fired. I further discovered the money being collected by forcing KSC employees to recycle for the state was not going to the state treasury, but to a private account called the Foundation Scholarship Fund. This fund represented the fiscal reserves that KSC was using to demonstrate to the Nebraska state legislature that it would be a financial asset to the university system.

According to the then current KSC physical plant director, Tom Jones, "all aluminum cans found on campus are state property and therefore cannot be recycled by students, student groups, or private groups." (This directive was a campus wide memo that I was shown by a source who wishes to remain anonymous). Contemplating this directive for several days led me to formulate the following questions: When does a can of soda that I purchase on campus become state property? Clearly I am buying both the aluminum can as well as its liquid contents when a purchase is made. Thus, the aluminum can would be my property until I chose to throw it into a KSC trash receptacle. This thought led to an additional insight and question: If aluminum cans found on the KSC campus are state property, then would not the money from recycling these cans collectively belong to the citizens of Nebraska? If this is in fact the correct legal conclusion to who owns these aluminum cans, then the money from recycling should therefore go to the Nebraska state treasury and not the KSC Foundation. I published this investigation as a letter to the Editor in the KSC student paper, *The Antelope* (either in November or December 1990, but I no longer have copies of this publication to check the date), and a private paper devoted to raising awareness on social and environmental issues called *The Weather* (Schroll, 1990).

The results of publishing my investigation proved the power of the press. Although it was never publicly acknowledged, I found out through my sources that KSC amended its policy on aluminum cans to reflect my conclusion. I also found out through my sources that physical plant director Tom Jones was (to put it in politically correct terms) not pleased with the results of my investigative journalism. Beyond all this, the confirmation that my conclusions had been sound and adopted was when I was invited by KSC's administration in the spring of 1991 to be part of a group of students and faculty whose task was to help create a scholarship program funded by recycling aluminum cans for students involved in research contributing toward raising awareness of what we can do to solve the eco-crisis.

The Far Reaching Social and Economic Consequences

Continuing to reflect on this confirmation that aluminum cans and all of the revenue generated by recycling them are the collective income of the citizens in Nebraska led me to a more far reaching insight. All recyclables (glass, tin, solid waste, etc) should be considered the collective wealth of every citizen in every city and state. On a personal level we are all free to dispose of recyclables in any way we choose, and it should be the right of any citizen to collect these recyclables in any way they choose. Beyond this in terms of any kind of systematic process of recycling, the revenue generated by recycling could then be redistributed to citizens. This redistribution could be done in a number of ways. Since it is a requirement of property owners in cities to pay for sanitation removal the revenue generated from recyclables could be used to pay for this service. If after this there would be additional revenue, this could be used to pay property taxes, which in turn would raise money for schools. Additional revenue beyond this could be used to pay for the energy consumption of electric utilities, help to fund public transportation, and so on. Moreover, affluent members of society could be given the option of receiving these benefits or donating this revenue back to the state and receiving a tax credit for their donation.

Some of you may wonder why I included "solid waste" in this list of recyclables. Do I mean composting? Composting is of course a step in the right direction toward utilizing solid waste and it should certainly be used for this. But there is also another use for solid waste when it is unable to be composted. Solid waste can be compressed and transformed into fuel pellets that can be burned like coal with fewer CO_2 emissions. As you have already guessed in reading this, using solid waste in this way would also help alleviate the build-up of CO_2 emissions in the atmosphere that are contributing to global climate change. It is also well known decaying biomass and solid waste that are not able to be used for composting generates methane gases that are now also contributing to CO_2 in the atmosphere and thus global climate change. To transform this problem into a resource, every landfill could have a methane-capture device. This captured methane could then be used in its gaseous form like natural gas to heat our homes, and it could be super-cooled into liquid form as a fuel for cars, trucks, and so on.

Conclusion

In this article I have hopefully shown that while transpesonal ecosophy appears to be an esoteric perspective, its influence on consciousness, attitudes, and resulting ways of being that influence our behavior produces practical consequences toward addressing the eco-crisis. Moreover in illustrating one of many activities that serve to create within us an awareness of transpersonal ecosophy (i.e., my unintended vision quest and eight day wilderness experience in Daniel Boon National Forest), this article provided a means of addressing the problem of global climate change and demonstrating practical solutions toward the creation of a sustainable culture. I look forward to all of us working together to make the vision of a sustainable culture a reality.

References

Fox, W. (1990). *Toward a transpersonal ecology: Developing new foundations for environmentalism.* Boston: Shambhala.

Metzner, R. (1999). *Green psychology: Transforming our relationship to the earth.* Rochester, VT: Park Street Press.

Schroll, M. A. (1990). State funds wasted on KSC recycling program. *The Weather,* Dec, 3.

Schroll, M. A. (2009). New science, new culture manifesto: Transpersonal ecosophy's vision of what it means to be human. *Association for Humanistic Psychology-Perspective,* June/July, 8-10.

Schroll, M. A. (2011). Editor's introduction: From primordial anthropology to a transpersonal ecosophy. *Anthropology of Consciousness, 22* (1), 4-8.

Tart, C. T. (1975). *States of consciousness.* New York: Dutton.

MARK A. SCHROLL, Ph.D., Research Adjunct Faculty, Institute of Transpersonal Psychology, Palo Alto, California, and serves on the Advisory Board of *Alternative Therapies in Health and Medicine.* He served as Guest Managing Editor of the special *Anthropology of Consciousness, 22*(1), 2011 issue "From Primordial Anthropology to a Transpersonal Ecosophy", and *Anthropology of Consciousness, 16*(1), 2005 issue "Primordial Visions in an Age of Technology". He co-chaired the 2009 "Bridging Nature and Human Nature" annual Society for the Anthropology of Consciousness conference co-sponsored by the Association for Transpersonal Psychology. He serves on the Editorial Board of *Paranthropology: Journal of Anthropological Approaches to the Paranormal.* He serves on the Windbridge Institute Scientific Advisory Board. He was the Founding Editor of *Rhine Online: Psi-News Magazine.* He Edited *Rhine Online, 3*(1), 2011, the special 2nd-anniversary issue "Sacred Sites, Consciousness, and the Eco-Crisis". He serves on the Editorial Board of *Goddess Thealogy: An International Journal for the Study of Feminism and Religion* and the Board of the Institute for Thealogy and Deasophy. He has been invited to serve as the Co-Editor of the 1st issue of *Goddess Thealogy* with Patricia 'Iolana (In Press). Schroll is a transpersonal cultural theorist and conference organizer with multi-disciplinary interests ranging from philosophy of science to transpersonal ecosophy. Contact: rockphd4@yahoo.com

Much More Than a Movement: The Parallel History of the Green Movement & Horticultural Therapy in the United States since the 1970s

Meredith Ball, LCSW

Ball, M.. (2011). Much more than a movement: The parallel history of the Green Movement & Horticultural Therapy in the United States since the 1970s. *Restoration Earth: An Interdisciplinary Journal for the Study of Nature & Civilization*, *1*(1), 84–86.

Abstract

The parallels between the resurgence of the green movement and the birth of Horticultural Therapy in the 1970s through present day are too similar to ignore. While the green movement has its roots in ancient history, the 1970s birthed a feverish response and call to action worthy of exploration. At the same time horticultural therapy re-emerged to answer a deeper reason for this green trend, which this paper will explore.

What Might Have Caused This Green Push?

After decades of industrialization and mass production, the 1970s bought about people's desires to literally reconnect with their roots. It was during this time that we saw the start of hippie communes, now called intentional communities, with the focus on ecological living (Schabner, 2004), an idea that has continued to flourish post 1970s. Emerging in the 1980s, local farming programs known as "Community Supported Agriculture" (CSA) began to emerge in the United States and today there are estimated 3,000 CSAs in the US (Local Harvest, 2011). Al Gore kept the green momentum going through the 1990s when he gathered legislators from 42 different countries to create the "Global Marshall Plan" for countries to grow in sustainable ways (Maranto, 1992). The new millennium has spanned the spectrum from states considering the banning of plastic bags to moratoriums on oil drilling.

While the rebirth of the green movement was beginning, the National Council for Therapy and Rehabilitation Through Horticulture was formed in 1975 (later titled the American Horticultural Therapy Association) to establish Horticultural Therapy (HT) as a profession with standards, support, a mission, and vision (American Horticultural Therapy Association [AHTA], 2007). The similar timing of the green resurgence and the formation of the AHTA was not coincidental.[1] Rather the two were a reflection of the deeper need for this trend of mutual healing that has continued to grow throughout the past four decades with no signs of stopping. This deeper need resulted from the prior decades where the vastness of industrialization usurped our natural resources. Further, the US experienced an increasing enormity of despair during and after the Vietnam War, which depleted our souls. The natural result was for people to look backwards to their roots and to seek a reconnection with the earth. The natural rhythm of life, living, and compassion are all reflected in nature—whether it be a forest of pine trees, the ocean tides, or the first flower of spring. The simplicity and beauty of nature was needed to heal our souls and bring meaning back to our lives, as Deloria Vine (1970) writes:

> Wilderness transformed into city streets, subways, giant buildings, and factories resulted in the complete substitution of the real world for the artificial world of the real man....Surrounded by an artificial universe when the warning signals are not the shape of the sky, the cry of the animals, the changing of seasons, but the simple flashing of the traffic light and the wail of an ambulance and police car, urban people have not idea what the natural verse is like. (p. 185)

The Emergence of Horticultural Therapy

The 1970s bore witness to people who turned to the slower paces of nature to slow down their lives. People turned to the healing powers of nature to heal their lives. People turned to the strength and resilience of nature to grow in their own lives. People needed nature more than ever to love, to nurture, to remind them how to nurture and love themselves. The disconnect between people and their literal roots due to the explosive growth of technology and urban sprawl created a profound desire for a reconnection to the natural healing world. Rebecca Haller, HTR, (2010) states: "planting a seed is the ultimate act of optimism" (personal communication). People needed to start planting seeds again. The profession of HT in the mid-1970s too felt this need for healing from people. The AHTA was formed and HT spread slowly, but consistently both through the establishment of an academic journal (Journal of Therapeutic Horticulture [1986–to present]) to promote research into the numerous HT programs and how they improve clients' social, cognitive, emotional and physical wellbeing; and through applied programs that have increased in number throughout the United States for populations of all ages and needs. And with these two developments a clear definition of what HT is was defined: "...a process through which plants, gardening activities, and the innate closeness we all feel toward nature are used as vehicles in professionally conducted programs of therapy and rehabilitation" (Davis, 1994).

HT programs developed designed to work with a range of populations of clients including children, teenagers, adults, and older adults, as well as people with physical, emotional, and social challenges (Simson & Strauss, 1998). Several programs have emerged such as: (a) the Cooper Riis (2011) program in North Carolina helping adults to improve their mental health and functioning; (b) Glass Gardens at the Rusk Institute (2011) in New York, which began in the 1970s to become a leader in the HT community, helping people to improve emotionally and physically; and (c) the work of Heather Benson (personal communication, September 27, 2010) who just completed a successful HT program for children with grief issues in the Tenderloin School District. Each of these programs highlights how HT is making differences with a variety of populations.

HT works by helping people heal while they engage in activities that also promote the healing of nature—a complete act of mutual healing. Research by Millet (2009) demonstrated how an HT program could be utilized to support the return to work and healing of clients struggling with burnout and chronic fatigue through the process of learning how to plant and garden. Pfeffer et al. (2009) demonstrated how HT programs could substantially improve the quality of life for clients with physical and mental challenges through specific gardening activities; while Wagenfeld's (2009) research demonstrated how HT could be successfully utilized to assist children with sensory challenges via garden activities. Bradley et al. (1998) demonstrated their HT program could help at-risk youth to return to school or work through garden activities. With the continuing development of HT programs within the US (and abroad) and their application, HT has been consistently demonstrating their robustness as a viable therapeutic intervention with enormous healing potential, both for the individual and the natural environment.

Breathing, Horticultural Therapy as the Air of the Green Movement

Just as the lives of clients who have received HT have been transformed, the green movement has offered healing to people seeking improvement in their quality of life. The going green movement, just like the growth of HT, has had a larger urgency for people to show the earth and each other our values of compassion, respect, and kindness. As people began to see the difference made for the earth, and for people with the experience of HT, as well as with simple acts of going green, the meaning of this movement grew

---

1 Please note that for the purposes of this article, the history of HT and the green movement in the US will be explored. Future articles will look at HT in various countries and those countries' organizations such as Thrive, founded in the UK in 1978, the Korean Horticultural Therapy Association founded in Asia in the 1980s, and the Canadian Horticultural Therapy Association founded in 1987.

deeper. The movement became, not simply sustainability, but recognition that in helping to heal the earth we could reclaim our humanity, our resilience, and our innate desire and need to continue life on this beautiful planet. People jumped on the green movement trail to prove we could be as strong and resilient as other creatures of nature. With HT and with the over-arching green movement that sparked its re-emergence, people manifest a firm mission and commitment to heal each other and the earth.

HT has been there all along, with Horticultural Therapists and their clients knowing the mutual healing that may come from plant and nature activities. HT may be thought of as the air of the green movement, helping us to breathe easier, find meaning in our lives, and move us to the next level of healing.

References

American Horticultural Therapy Association (AHTA). (2007). "Definitions and positions. Retrieved on June 10, 2010, from http://www.ahta.org/documents/Final_HT_Position_Paper_updated_409.pdf.

Bradley, E.L., et. al. (1998). Non-Traditional, experimental horticultural programs for at-risk Youth. In M.D. Burchett, J. Tarran, & R. Wood (Eds.), *Towards a new millennium in people–plant relationships* (pp. 381–383). Sydney: University of Technology.

Cooper Riis, Inc. (2011). "Cooper Riis: A Healing Community." Retrieved on July 2, 2011, from http://www.cooperriis.org/difference/staffpages/staff_lifeskills.html.

Davis, S. (April 19, 1994). Ninth annual congressional initiatives and awards ceremonies. Washington, DC: Senate Russell Office Building.

Local Harvest (2011). "Community Supported Agriculture". Retrieved on July 2, 2011, from http://www.localharvest.org/csa/.

Maranto, G. (February, 9, 1992) "Saving Ourselves". New York Times.

Millet, P. (2009). "Integrating horticulture into the vocational rehabilitation process of individuals with fatigue, Chronic Fatigue, and burnout: A theoretical model". Journal of Therapeutic Horticulture, XIX, 10–23.

Pfeffer, J., et al. (2009). "Survey of horticultural therapy programs in Tennessee". Journal of Therapeutic Horticulture, XIX, 24–29.

Rusk Institute. (2011). "Glass Gardens". Retrieved on August 1, 2011 from http://www.med.nyu.edu/glassgardens/.

Schabner, D. (July 22, 2004). "'60s generation and their offspring still working for a change". ABC News. Retrieved on July 2, 2011 from http://abcnews.go.com/US/story?id=96711&page=1.

Simson, S. & Straus, M. (1998). Horticulture as therapy: Principles and practice. Florida: CRC Press.

Vine, D. (1970). We talk you listen. New York: Delta.

Wagenfeld, A. (2009). "It's more than seeing green: Exploring the senses through gardening". Journal of Therapeutic Horticulture, XIX, 46–53.

MEREDITH BALL is a Licensed Clinical Social Worker and aspiring Horticultural Therapist in Claremont, CA. Her MSW, earned at Bryn Mawr Graduate School of Social Work and Social Research, Bryn Mawr, PA, concentrated a focus on advocacy, planning and program development. Horticultural Therapy is the culmination of her passion for nature and an understanding of macro community needs acquired from education and work experience. Meredith has seen hundreds of clients benefit from the mutual healing of horticultural therapy activities and looks forward to assisting in further promoting the integration of this profession into a variety of health settings.

Learning from Leaves:

Transformational Ecopsychology

Mark Morton Glasgow

Glasgow, M. M. (2011). Learning from leaves: Transformational ecopsychology *Restoration Earth: An Interdisciplinary Journal for the Study of Nature & Civilization, 1*(1), 87–94. Copyright © The Authors. All rights reserved. For reprint information contact: oceanseminary@verizon.net.

Introduction

What madness is ours that moves us to destroy the world we live in, other species, and other human beings? What fury has provoked such violent and unwarranted destruction of nature? Has human-generated violence irreparably damaged the reciprocal cause–effect informational loop between our genetics and the environment? Can we halt the damage or better yet, reverse it? It seems unexplainable from any rational viewpoint and gives pause to consider why it is happening and if we can stop it. These provocative questions warrant a new awareness, and above all, practicable solutions if we are to avoid an apocalyptic, environmental nightmare largely of our own making. There is a solution, one that teaches a simple method of consciously reconnecting with nature, called the Natural Systems Thinking Process (NTSP), developed by Ecopsychologist, Dr. Michael J. Cohen. The following excerpt from the book *Peace Is Every Step: The Path of Mindfulness in Everyday Life* (Hanh, 1992) speaks to the heart and mind of anyone familiar with NTSP:

> I asked the leaf whether it was frightened because it was autumn and the other leaves were falling. The leaf told me, "No. During the whole spring and summer I was completely live. I worked hard to help nourish the tree, and now much of me is in the tree. I am not limited by this form. I am also the whole tree, and when I go back to the soil, I will continue to nourish the tree. So I don't worry at all. As I leave this branch and float to the ground, I will wave to the tree and tell her, "I will see you again very soon." That day there was a wind blowing and after a while, I saw the leaf leave the branch and float down to the soil, dancing joyfully, because as it floated it saw itself already there in the tree. It was so happy. I bowed my head, knowing that I have a lot to learn from the leaf. (p. 17)

According to Dossey and Muller, Cohen has provided an environmentally sound, hands-on educational tool that consciously reconnects us to the often ignored source of spirit and wellness found in nature (as cited in Cohen, 2003, pg. i). The course description promises to educate participants in mastering the therapeutic science of Applied Ecopsychology. By learning to create moments that let the Earth teach, the course assures increased individual, social and environmental wellbeing. This restorative thinking skill claims to strengthen more than 50 natural senses to embrace their nurturing origins in the balanced, self-correcting, and renewing ways of nature within and around us.

In contrast with NSTP, much scholarship in ecology is rife with politics far-removed from the field. Nature and ecology occupy yet another battleground fought over by those with political, philosophical, and religious axes to grind (Soper, 1995; Biro, 2005). Surprisingly, the simple word *nature* amasses sixty-six different meanings (Lovejoy, 1978), not one arising from nature proper. Defining nature summons impulsive and often contrary stances based on one's academic, political, or religious viewpoint. Intellectual historian David N. Livingstone (1995) outlines three ways of representing nature, so "we can begin to *cut a path through this forbidding terrain*" (italics mine, p. 353). Language too, has become the subject of analysis to discover how literature influences and reflects the exchange between humanity and the biosphere (Bennett & Royle, 2009). Although such approaches may serve to identify and characterize our descent to madness, one might question the value of explaining such madness without resolving it. This is why Cohen's approach offers a solution to all who have ever seriously entertained the idea that nature has a voice and wisdom to share. NSTP encourages us to pause, while listening carefully to leaves until finally we register their teaching.

This author took the on-line course with a group of students from three different continents. By nature, an open-minded skeptic trained in the scientific method, he wants to answer the question: does the course live up to its hype? In reviewing student participation, a precourse survey defined each student's motives for taking the course. Those survey responses provided a benchmark for later deciding if the course had satisfied those motivational needs. The course content, the literature, and especially comments made by participants in their weekly assignments, all suggested a revitalizing, more conscious connection to nature, ourselves, and others is possible.

What motivates one to learn from leaves by adopting NSTP? Several motivations come to mind: the need for change, alienation from nature, a need for healing, and social problems. Sustainable development, for example, now attracts increasing attention worldwide, due much in thanks, to Al Gore, the Nobel Prize and Emmy–Award winning, former vice-president. Gore's message in the Academy Award-winning documentary, *An Inconvenient Truth*, was a wake-up call for many of us. Previously, many considered environmental issues and sustainable development as the nerdy fodder of futurist scientists, think-tank technocrats, and Greenpeace activists. However, this is no longer the case; fuelled by the growing concern over the impact of global warming, sustainable development has now become a fashionable topic. This need for global change mirrors the need for personal change expressed in comments made by students in their first assignment:

> I had resigned from 35 years in the corporate world. I resigned because I had decided that I would rather starve than continue working there.
>
> I decided that I was a square peg trying to fit into a round hole and decided that it was time to find more fulfilling work.
>
> The young boy, now a young man living in a big city had made his acquaintance with fear, pain and the stressful sense of feeling alone and isolated.
>
> With each decade that passes it is clear that we have become more and more disconnected from our source. From the foods we eat to the video games assimilating outdoor activities our children play there has never been a stronger need to give humans a tool to open up to the beautiful intelligence that surrounds us in nature.

The sense of alienation from nature, ourselves, and others, ranks high in motivating participants seeking a resolution to their growing sense of estrangement from the natural world. The notion of alienation is unusual because it impels an effort to explain a widespread, subjective and often indefinable feeling, while critiquing any society that regularly produces it (Graeber, n.d.). What is indisputable is the connection between feeling alienated and the experience of living in an increasingly urbanized, impersonal, and industrialized environment. The destructive social effects are also undeniable: depression, anxiety, hopelessness, substance abuse, broken marriages, co-dependency, consumerism, violence, and suicide. Again, we find a correlation between the macro and micro, reflected in the following comments:

> Although I am "successful" by societal standards, I feel disconnected, of little value, alone, and unhappy.
>
> I am spiritless in a corporate environment. Lies are truths. Truths are lies. Depression results.
>
> Cut off from his root he felt dead to himself, dead to others and numb to the world.
>
> There were shadows of random violence and substance abuse in our home, leftovers from the generational trauma and displacement of my mother's ancestors.
>
> I too, have suffered the feelings of alienation you mention and like you, I realize that to save others; we must first save ourselves.
>
> Only by making a genuine reconnect to nature, will such materially motivated, consumer oriented addicts have the opportunity to regain their mental and emotional health.
>
> Our culture's nature-conquering stories cut us off.
>
> Appallingly, most children are beaten by their parents when they are very young to make them obedient. My abusive parent had such rage, and for a child to sense this rage, they assume the abusive parent wants them gone yes and the child also feels somehow responsible.

Healing is another aim of ecopsychology; one that everyone sometimes needs. When trying to help people, healers must understand their patients' histories, the terrain within which they live, and their ethical duty to do no harm. Interestingly, in the Native American Okanagan language, each syllable of the four syllable word for *insanity* communicates a significantly ecopsychological circumstance, which signals a disconnection from the web of life (Rozak, 1995; Conn, 2005; Cohen, 2005). According to Conn, the syllables

have the following meanings:
1. 1st syllable: "talk, talk inside your head" (p. 533)
2. 2nd syllable: "scattered and having no community" (p. 534)
3. 3rd syllable: "having no relationship to the land" (p. 534)
4. 4th syllable: "being disconnected from the whole-earth part" (p. 534)

A study undertaken by the Canadian government highlighted the effect of rapid social change on the mental and physical health of its citizens (LaLonde, 1981). According to the study, technological innovation caused some of the social change. However, changing social values stressing private pleasure over commitment to the common good resulted in significant disorientation and alienation. Of particular interest was the finding that increased levels of disorientation and alienation led to serious health outcomes. Thirty years later, the disturbing status quo under which the Earth and its inhabitants now suffer remains unchanged. Student comments communicate their sense of personal loss mixed with the hope that conscious contact with nature can reverse their alienation from nature and others:

> Nature is forever true to its purpose and always confirms the way. When the mind becomes still, the heart speaks and nature confirms.
>
> I think that people can speak and listen to words endlessly without it having as much influence on them as a single experience.
>
> No doubt words offer an enigma when removed from the heart; they support the materially conditioned mind's ability to divide us from the vital aspects of our being.
>
> My greatest comforted moments have all been non verbal…It took me years of telling the story of some of these experiences to integrate them fully. But the experiences themselves, those moments when life stops, and then goes on again in a totally different way, were all non verbal.
>
> Webstrings test the limits of my powers of description to the point where I am left outside of language and feel my five-legged ego dissolving into the apprehended.
>
> We are in dire need for contact with each other and with other living things.
>
> Community is not something to be taken lightly. It is built and maintained by deeply and profoundly respecting its right to exist along with the human and nonhuman entities that make it up.
>
> Dear L, M & R, Today, you guys made me weep but the weeping was not from brokenness, it was from wholeness. Thank you and I commit to all of you again and again and again….
>
> I appreciate that you expressed to D. your sadness in her leaving. And that you are able to express to M. a webstring of attachment for him to be here in the group with us.
>
> First let me thank you for your continued support…it buttresses my resolve and draws me ever more closely into the bosom of our fledgling community, consciously binding me to the beauty of all who voluntarily reside here.
>
> Thank you for being present and redeeming my sense of hope that we, as human beings, will look into the mirror to know who is responsible for the current state of things.
>
> This gratitude reminded me of when I first stepped on the land of my farm as a visitor… I felt such happiness; I felt that the land welcomed me.
>
> When we moved here the land had been brutalized and stripped of all topsoil; it was so sterile that not even a lizard was left alive.
>
> When I am lying on the ground, looking at the sky, I am part of an amazing part of a part of a part…
>
> Ignoring the right of all nature, animate or inanimate to be accorded the respect I would like to receive, threatens webstrings, individual and collective well-being.
>
> The heartbreaking reality is that modern society has desensitized these natural attractions to the point that most of the people I meet *are so out of touch with this wisdom within them* that they have become addicted to destructive habits.
>
> Webstrings are expressions beginning and ending with me incorporating all that is.

While unsustainable exploitation threatens the planet's ecological health, the number of psychologically disturbed people occupying the planet is on the rise (Brown, 1995). Sadly, comments from the course participants mirror Brown's statement:

> Last year I was asked to go to another city to assume the role of manager of a facility as the manager was being let go. When I arrived I saw a group of wounded broken people.
>
> His pain was intense, his mind bothersome and that former connection with nature had almost died. Cut off from his root he felt dead to himself, dead to others and numb to the world.
>
> Many people live in fear of the future, of the state of the environment etc. I know some activists that are so scared that they are not doing anything!
>
> In other words I was defining myself by what I had accomplished. I really didn't have a clue who I was. When I got right down to it I discovered that I was miserable, had been struggling with a lot of depression and fatigue but compensated by doing "things' well. The contradiction of living like that was exhausting.
>
> Children are forced to accept very early that these cruel acts were normal, harmless, and even good for us. No other species inflicts such cruelty on its offspring. It's no wonder that our individual and collective relationships are so fraught with violence and abuse.

What are the irrational forces that attract people to their personal and environmental bad habits? Are the individual self and psyche, as some have suggested, developmentally linked in some matrixian manner to become Self and Psyche? Does healing depend on a conscious reconnection with nature that transports us beyond the narcissistic fascination we have developed with the notion of I, me, and mine? These are captivating questions; questions that NSTP may be able to answer based on the following student comments:

> This metamorphosis of human arrogance and greed into nature's impartial benevolence requires much more than anything we have in our philosophy; it requires a direct injection of new knowledge and understanding.
>
> When I go out into nature, I go with an open mind, admitting that I know nothing. In my humility, I can surrender and accept the teachings that are offered. I return home knowing something that I did not previously.
>
> Being part of the group impacts my physiology of relationship, when I read your process, and join my own to your learning— I feel soothed, and companioned in the same way I do in nature.
>
> Finally, his early experiments affirmed the value of NSTP's potential, reminding him of his direct participation in the flow of life.
>
> I trust Nature will attract my consciousness to verbalize webstrings in a way that others will know the value of Natural Systems Thinking Process.
>
> I grew a layer in trust of nature to meet both my physical and emotional needs. I grew a layer of belief in my life purpose.
>
> I realized that my self-worth can either be enhanced or diminished by my trustfulness or distrust of nature, the more authentic my degree of trustfulness, the greater my sense of self-worth.
>
> In one flash of nature catalyzed insight, I immediately sense nature's beckoning call like the prodigal son too long separated from his birthright.

Recent research in neurology and cardio-neurology highlights the social toll caused by violence and neglect in early childhood. Studies have found emotional deprivation in the early formative period of childhood results in specific and seemingly immutable compromises in neural anatomy and physiology (Pearce, 2005). Compounding these findings, further research suggests grown men from a neglected childhood were unresponsive to forming positive personal connections, implying a lifetime of social isolation and emotional poverty (Pearce, 2004). Research with mammals shows a link between any mammal's emotional state during conception and gestation and the quality and characteristics of her progeny. Biochemical and molecular research have shown that all biological organisms, including humans, share the will to survive. This fundamental survival drive, referred to as a "biological imperative" is intrinsic to every living organism (Lipton, 1998).

Researchers have subdivided the drive to survive into two physiological categories: behaviors supporting growth and those supporting protection (Lipton, Bensch & Karasek, 1991). Growth-related behaviors include those associated with seeking nutrients and sympathetic environments for individual survival and those associated with seeking mates for species survival. Protection behaviors include those employed by organisms to avoid harm. Interestingly, studies of molecular control mechanisms suggest that when forced to protect itself, an organism's growth pathways suspend. In human beings, this behavior occurs as the organism senses the negative, flight or fight extreme of the two polarities fittingly described as love and fear (Lipton, 1998). Lipton correctly points to a new vision which involves "turning away from the Darwinian notion of the 'survival of the fittest' and adopting a new credo, 'survival of the most loving!'" (p. 10). Student comments seem to indicate that nature nurtures when parents cannot:

> I too share a painful childhood history that drove me outdoors early in my life, vestiges of the difficulties my own parents faced growing up in their own birth families. I too found in the natural world greater comfort, warmth and solace than was available at home.
>
> The woods, the ocean, the sky and the earth itself were therefore more of a family to me than my own family.
>
> It is undeniable, the experience of reconnecting with nature, soothes the hurt child within, now an angry adult, who disassociated from the original cause, expresses their feelings of anger, helplessness, despair, longing, anxiety, and pain in destructive acts against, the natural world or against themselves.
>
> My home life was stable and solid, and had random, deep violence as part of a "discipline" structure. So I felt safer outside.

Besides what motivates one seeking wellness through restoring their connection with nature as taught in NSTP, it would be interesting to assess outcomes. Conn (2005), defines the theoretical base underpinning ecopsychology as one which recognizes the earth as a living organism in which human beings, their psyches, and cultures are an integral part. The author, in framing the scope of applied ecopsychology, further recognizes the interdependent and interconnected needs of both earth and humans. Any consideration of the impact of nature on health must consider E.O. Wilson's Biophilia Theory that human beings feel innately attracted to other living organisms (St Leger, 2003). This idea has broadened to suggest human health and well-being may depend on our connection to nature (Robinson, 2009; Frumkin, 2001; Cohen, 2003; Jordan, 2009). Multiple studies signal the positive impact on the human need for nature stimulated by the positive influence the natural world has on our emotional, psychological, and spiritual development (Maller, Townsend, Pryor, Brown, & St Leger, 2005). NSTP teaches how to reestablish our place in the natural world by engaging our fifty-three senses in consciously reconnecting with nature. According to Cohen (2007), natural ecosystems "compost and transform industrial society's pollution of our mind and body into personal, environmental and spiritual well-being" (back cover). Student comments reflected positive outcomes by practicing NSTP:

> Although I experienced the connection with nature I never *realized that nature was within me and part of me.*
>
> My encounters with nature have always left me recharged, reintegrated and once again able to deal with the unnatural world that gave impetus to my nature-seeking ways.
>
> To realise *fully* that we are all connected by and to the same webstrings will vastly improve our understanding and acceptance of each other.
>
> I suppose nature, true to its nature, embraces all of us, and for me, its intervention in my life was crucial in my taking more responsibility for my choices. It allowed me to acknowledge that my wishes could be transformed into reality, in the form of a reconstructed home and family.
>
> Repeating the exercise of taking time to connect to nature when I am outdoors is training me to note webstrings to sounds, colors, smells, textures, shapes, motion, warmth, cold, touch…I am filled with the attractions and become more aware, still, calm, connected, safe, inspired, confident, compassionate.
>
> Undoubtedly, change will be necessary to undo the damage done by a lifetime of nature-disconnected activity. You are correct in realizing that by reconnecting to nature in a natural way, all that is necessary to heal, will in due time, be revealed.

A unique feature of NSTP is its practice as part of a global network, linked by the modern technology of the world-wide-web. Cohen's greening of technology, offers a growing ecological community, diverse opportunities including hands-on, Biophilia-in-action, classes, research, scholarships, earth-friendly jobs, careers, internships, and teaching certifications. For those of more academic bent, there are courses and both undergraduate and graduate degree programmes. All are available on-line and scholarships are available for those who need them. The global outreach of Cohen's initiative clearly distinguishes his work and resolves the major challenge of integrating what one has learned in nature on returning to society. Cohen's vision has extended to planting green virtual communities, linking individuals studying on courses offered by *Project NatureConnect* at the Institute of Global Education, a special non-governmental organization (NGO) consultant to UNESCO.

In closing, the author, a naturopath and educator, who has practiced yoga for more than 30 years, felt struck by the following:

> Nature has a powerful role to play in transformative healing work.
> Nature offers a superior therapeutic setting to work conducted indoors.
> Ritual is an important and vital element when working with nature.
> An intrinsic respect for nature is a prerequisite for healing to occur.
> The Natural Systems Thinking Process includes all of the above and promotes intrapersonal, interpersonal and environmental well-being.

Finally, it would be thoughtless not to give my esteemed colleagues the last say and it is to them, I wish to dedicate this article:

> There is power in the process, great healing and as we remediate damaged webstrings, we, others and the world at-large are all benefited.
> The feeling of coming home into nature is one that I definitely want more of.
> Thank you for revealing the webstrings binding us in mutual attraction. Your ability to mirror my experiences from a distance creates harmonic resonance and provides a palpable therapeutic effect evidenced in the way I feel.
> Bathed in attraction to nature's beauty, poised between the sense world and the world of feeling and thinking, I find myself at rest.
> Being grateful in nature is creating change from the bottom up.
> I am learning how to consciously participate in natural systems, including relationships with other people, in life enhancing ways.
> In opening up to and sensing the greater world of web-stringed intelligence, we harness the wisdom of the whole, while mirroring it in our intra-personal and inter-personal relationships.
> Consistently reconnecting with nature, restores vitality, improves disposition and makes life worth living.
> Conscious participation is possible through feedback from webstring intelligence; the intelligence of natural senses. These senses are delicate and can be desensitized to the extent that they no longer work. Natural senses can be enhanced by learning to listen and obey them.
> I suddenly see that Nature actually communicated with me through my various senses and *told me what she needed* in a way that was as real as any worded language.
> There were grasses on a hill that were swaying in the breeze. I would watch them and rock slowly back and forth to their rhythm. The different colors and lengths reminded me that we are all different but can all be rocked by mother earth if we have awareness.
> I was constantly working on myself using the views from this window to receive the gifts of peace and comfort and then I would turn away from the window and pass these gifts on to my (dying) cousin and a couple of the people who were there a lot as well.
> When I consciously connect through Nature with the world at-large, peace, harmony and unity result.
> I love this pond because it vibrates with life. I love myself because I vibrate with   life.
> I love this place because it exudes a beautiful calm that seeps into every pore of my skin until it takes over my whole being. I love myself because I exude a beautiful calm that seeps into every pore of my skin until it takes over my whole being.
> I love these trees because they are tall, overcome challenging placement and still thrive, share, create community and remain whole. I love myself because I am tall, overcome challenging placement and still thrive, create community and remain whole.

I am attracted to Ivy because of its teaching ability. I like myself because of my teaching ability. Little drops of water wear away the stone and collectively, introducing this practice into our lives and into the lives of others, we can and will change the tide of history.

Note: This article was the final assignment in the graduate course, *Psychological Elements of Global Citizenship*, offered by Akamai University, Portland State University, and Project NatureConnect. Directed by Dr. Michael J. Cohen, the coursework and collection of data occurred between August and October of 2010. During this time, five students and a graduate assistant from three continents learned how excessive separation from nature stresses our sensuous inner nature leading to personal and global troubles. Students learned to reverse this destructive cycle by mastering thoughtful sensory nature reconnecting skills that dissolve stress by satisfying their deepest natural loves, wants, and spirit. The hands-on course teaches leadership, counseling, and mental health skills that feelingly tap the higher power of the Earth's wisdom. Students sent weekly email assignments to every member of the group, for response. The email contacts empowered students to let nature help them nurture improved rapport, wellness, and responsibility on both personal and global levels. All comments included in this article are with permission of the participants and the author has removed any identifying personal information to preserve confidentiality.

References

Bennett, A., & Royle, N. (2009). Eco. In *An introduction to literature, criticism and theory* (pp. 155–168). Harlow, United Kingdom: Pearson.

Biro, A. (2005). *Denaturalizing ecological politics: Alienation from nature from Rousseau to the Frankfort School and beyond.* Toronto, Canada: University of Toronto Press.

Brown, L. R. (1995). Ecopsychology and the environmental revolution: An environmental foreward. In T. Rozak, M. E. Gomes, & A. D. Kanner (Eds.), *Ecopsychology: Restoring the Earth healing the mind* (pp. xiii–xvi). San Francisco, CA: Sierra Club Books.

Cohen, M. J. (2003). *The Web of Life Imperative.* Victoria, Canada: Trafford Publishing.

Cohen, M. J. (2005). *The crisis identified in the Last Child in the Woods finds an adult remedy: Controversy flares as outdoor education introduces environmental sanity through Human-Nature Psychology.* Retrieved, October 2, 2010, from http://www.ecopsych.com/tapenvt.html

Cohen, M. J. (2007). *Reconnecting with nature: Finding wellness through restoring your bond with the Earth* (3 Ed.). Lakeville, MN: Ecopress.

Conn, S. A. (2005). Living in the Earth: Ecopsycholgy, health, and psychotherapy. In K. Fitzpatrick (Ed.), *Consciousness & healing: Integral approaches to Mind-Body Medicine* (pp. 530–541). St. Louis, MO: Elsevier.

Frumkin, H. (2001, April). Beyond toxicity: Human health and the natural environment. *American Journal of Preventive Medicine, 20*(3), 234.

Graeber, D. (n.d.). Alienation. Retrieved October 1, 2010, from http://science.jrank.org/pages/7480/Alienation.html

Guggenheim, D. (Director). (2006). An inconvenient truth: A global warning [DVD].

Hanh, T. N. (1992). *Peace is every step: Mindfulness in everyday life.* New York, NY: Bantam Books. Hollywood: Paramount.

Jordan, M. (2009, April). Back to nature. *Therapy Today,* 29–30. Retrieved October 1, 2010, from http://www.ecotherapy.org.uk/files/ecotherapy/home/Therapy_today_article_on_ecotherapy.pdf

LaLonde, M. (1981). *A new perspective on the health of Canadians: A working paper* (Working Paper). Retrieved September 25, 2010, from Health Canada: http://www.hc-sc.gc.ca/hcs-sss/pubs/system-regime/1974-lalonde/index-eng.php#a2

Lipton, B. H. (1998, October). Nature, nurture and the power of love. *Journal of Prenatal and Perinatal Psychology and Health, 13*(1), 3–10. Retrieved September 28, 2010, from http://birthpsychology.com/journal-issue/volume-13-issue-1

Lipton, B., Bensch, K. G., & Karasek, M. (1991). Microvesselendothelial cell transdifferentiation: Phenotypic characterization. *Differentiation, 46*, 117–133.

Livingstone, D. N. (1995, October). The polity of nature: Representation, virtue, strategy. *Cultural Geographies, 2*, 353. Retrieved September 18, 2010, from http://cgi.sagepub.com/content/2/4/353.full.pdf+html

Lovejoy, A. O. (1978). Nature as aesthetic norm. In *Essays in the history of ideas* (pp. 69–77). Baltimore, MD: John Hopkins University Press.

Maller, C., Townsend, M., Pryor, A., Brown, P., & St Leger, L. (2005, March). Healthy nature healthy people: 'contact with nature' as an upstream health promotion intervention for populations. *Health Promotion International, 21(1)*, 45-54. Retrieved October 2, 2010, from http://heapro.oxfordjournals.org/content/21/1/45.full.pdf+html

Pearce, J. C. (2004). *Nurturance: A biological imperative*. Retrieved September 18, 2010, from http://www.shiftinaction.com/node/107

Pearce, J. C. (2005). The conflict of biological and cultural imperatives. In K. Fitzpatrick (Ed.), *Consciousness & healing: Integral approaches to Mind–Body Medicine* (pp. 181–192). St. Louis, MO: Elsevier Health Sciences.

Robinson, L. (2009). Psychotherapy as if the world mattered. In L. Buzzell & C. Chalquist (Eds.), *Ecotherapy: Healing with nature in mind* (pp. 24–29). San Francisco, CA: Sierra Club Books.

Rozak, T. (1995, Spring). The greening of psychology: Exploring the ecological unconscious. *Gestalt Journal, 18*(1), 87-113. Retrieved September 25, 2010, from http://www.igjournal.org/guests/Roszak.pdf

Soper, K. (1995). *What is nature? Culture, politics and the non-human*. Brighton,   United Kingdom: Blackwell.

MARK GLASGOW, BSc, PgDip, MSc, MHSc, ND, OMD, PhD (Candidate) has forty-plus years of international experience spanning four continents. He has worked in government service, private companies, and nonprofit organizations, while teaching, supervising, managing and directing. His formal studies include a Bachelor of Science in Alternative Medicine, a Master of Health Sciences, and professional doctorates in Naturopathy and Oriental Medicine. He has lived in Italy, Saudi Arabia, and India where he studied Ayurveda under clinical conditions. He lives with his wife in the south of Brazil where he has taught Brazilian graduates and postgraduates for the past six years. Dr. Glasgow is studying Ecopsychology at Ocean Seminary College, while enrolled on a Master of Public Health and a PhD in Integrative Medicine at other institutions. His current research focuses on the interdisciplinary field of consciousness studies, especially the challenges faced by science of incorporating human consciousness within its model. His specific interest is the problem of integrating two seemingly disparate parts of material nature: subtle mind and gross matter. His applied research in energetic and informational medicine combines the phenomenological ontology of *Gaudīya Vaishnava Vedanta* and the new physics of macroscopic quantum mechanics.

Book Review: *Life Rules*

By Ellen LaConte
Green Horizon, 2010
ISBN: 978-1-4502-5918-7
283 pages, paperback, $21.95 ($9.99 ebook version available from iUniverse.com)
http://www.ellenlaconte.com/life-rules-the-book/

Remer, M. (2011). Book review: *Life rules*. Restoration Earth: An Interdisciplinary Journal for the Study of Nature & Civilization, 1(1), 95–96. Copyright © The Authors. All rights reserved. For reprint information contact: oceanseminary@verizon.net.

Earth is rapidly approaching a point of Critical Mass, the global economy is an insidious virus, and the way in which humans live on the planet has induced planetary conditions similar to the way in which AIDS works in the body. These are the main premises of the book, *Life Rules*, by Ellen LaConte. A manifesto for radical worldwide change, *Life Rules* asserts that Life has one main goal, "to last." To this end, "Life rules, we don't" and if we do not rapidly change our destructive habits, Life may well decide to get rid of us. LaConte asserts that humans feel as if they can live outside of the systemic boundaries and ecological rules of life. While this may have been possible during the last century, it is not sustainable and holds no future now. Earth is having an immune-system response to humanity's ecologically unsustainable habits and lifestyle and this response shows up in observable phenomenon like climate change.

"Other-than-human species provide for themselves and each other in ways that are truly sustainable and relatively equitable, and they organize themselves and relate to each other in ways that are organically democratic, or biocratic" (LaConte, 2010, p. 55). Our current economic system does not mimic the sustaining behaviors of Life; it mimics the behavior of a virulent disease. The author also notes that we cannot come up with global solutions, only Life itself is prepared to produce global solutions. LaConte points out significantly that, "there is no peak solar event anywhere on the horizon" (p. 125) and advocates a subsistence economy the functions according to "Life's Economic Survival Protocol" as do all other natural economies. Currently, we have a *viral economy*; it has to continue to grow. In a natural economy, "growth for its own sake is a sign of disease and perpetual growth is fatal" (p. 134).

We have the opportunity to rein in Critical Mass and to establish harmony with Life by becoming "Deep Green" in behavior and outlook, by welcoming in the "Ecozoic" age, and by embracing a "Biocracy." "To be Deeply Green would be *eco*logical, sustainable and embedded *in* rather than *larger* than Life. Lifeways that mimic Life's ways would *be* Deep—deeply—Green," (p. 181) rather than shopping, living, and consuming in the "weakly green" ways so many of us do today. Current Green initiatives are not enough and may lull us into a false sense of making change rather than the complete systemic overhaul that is truly required. Small steps like changing light bulbs do not meaningfully alter the status quo and "perhaps more insidiously, they give us hope" (p. 83).

The AIDS analogy, while initially effective, becomes at times tiresome and heavy-handed; and *Life Rules* places largest emphasis on the problems and wrongs in the world, rather than solutions. It is only when the reader arrives at the final third of the book where suggestions for what *to do* versus pronouncements about the hopeless condition of the planet emerge. This leaves the reader feeling discouraged and almost hopeless (indeed, LaConte writes "hope is for the weak and foolish!"[p. 83], suggesting that this in fact the intent of the author). For example, Part 1 of *Life Rules* is titled, "Why so much is going wrong and isn't getting fixed." In my own life, work, and teaching I believe we need to take the closest look at what is going *right* in order for healthy new conditions to flourish. Old problems don't survive in healthy new conditions and I would have liked to see more emphasis on the healthy new conditions desired. What we pay attention to is what we produce and we cannot just count the world's problems and then expect to be successful at addressing them. As it is, two thirds of the book focuses on the wrongs and problems and the final section starts to address what we can do about it.

LaConte's book is, however, a very sobering wake-up call even for the most ecologically and sustainable minded among us. Her work emphasizes that humans *must* live within Earth's means precisely because "penalties for breaking Life's rules are harsh. Extinction is one of them" (p. 55). In *Life Rules,* LaConte advocates community *economics* versus the global economy and taking lessons from bacteria and how they survive and thrive. In order to recover from Critical Mass, we need to choose harmony with Life's rules for sustainable, biological economies, we need a partnership model of living, collaboration with all species, and "we" thinking.

   Life Rules provides a new metaphor for conceptualizing the global climate crisis as one in which humans, with our social and economic practices that mimic that of a virus, have produced an associated crisis response in the immune system of the planet. While, as a reader, I would have preferred greater emphasis on present and future strategies for creating meaningful change, LaConte's passionate argument provides an important contribution to the field of literature exploring our current relationship to the earth.

—Molly Remer

Disclosure: I received a complimentary copy of this book for review purposes.

✣❈✣

MOLLY REMER, MSW, ICCE, CCCE, is a certified birth educator, writer, and activist. She is a professor of Human Services, an LLL Leader, editor of the Friends of Missouri Midwives newsletter, and a doctoral student at Ocean Seminary College. She has two wonderful sons and an infant daughter and she blogs about birth, motherhood, and women's issues at Talk Birth (http://talkbirth.wordpress.com)

"Lounging" copyright © 2011 by Anne Westlund. Photo taken in Washington State, USA.

Book Review: *Wild Way Home: Spiritual Life in the 3rd Millennium*

Collings, T. (2011). Book review: *Wild way home: Spiritual life in the 3rd millennium*. *Restoration Earth: An Interdisciplinary Journal for the Study of Nature & Civilization, 1*(1), 97–98. Copyright © The Authors. All rights reserved. For reprint information contact: oceanseminary@verizon.net.

by Alan Drengson
Lightstar Press, 2010
ISBN: 978-0-9205-7808-7
300 pages, paperback, $24.95

Alan Drengson's compelling book, *Wild Way Home: Spiritual Life in the 3rd Millennium* (2010), introduces a new spiritual discipline that is both personally fulfilling and ecologically sensitive. In the introduction, Drengson defines his Wild Way as a "Whole Art" that can help us become more balanced through present, intimate contact with the wild world that exists both outside and inside each of us. One of the key values of this book is its ability to inspire readers without using any fear-based apocalyptic preaching. Refreshingly, Drengson does not view civilization and nature as incommensurable. He explains that "the wild (rural) complements the tame (urban). Where they meet, we discover who we are" (p. 6). It is this balanced perspective that makes the Wild Way an effective, realistic method to rediscovering ourselves and interacting more sustainably with the natural world. The meat of this book is a detailed unpacking of the four life practice systems of the Wild Way: (a) spontaneous spirituality, (b) shamanic journeying and trance dancing, (c) formal movement disciplines, and (d) wild journeying (p. 15). Drengson uses personal stories and well developed metaphors to describe these life practice systems and how they can help us reconnect with our wild selves.

Wild Way Home does not glitter with Castaneda-like fantasies complete with the alien allure of manufactured mystery. This book is honest, clear, and relatable. We can all learn from these simple stories and follow these lifestyle practices. Drengson tells us about his experience with Heron, a powerful friend and teacher, who taught him the importance of a tribal community. We learn about respecting animals as "real beings, not abstractions" (p. 77) through stories about his cat Lucky. Balance can be attained through the simple practice of mindful walking as described in Drengson's hike to the peak of Mt. Douglas.

This wild power can be accessed wherever we are because "we have wild Nature within us" (p. 210). *Wild Way Home* is, in many ways, also a critique of modern industrial society. It warns us of the dangers of the mechanized consumer-centric monoculture to which many of us belong. The construction of the industrial complex hides our connection to our ecosystem, it makes us feel placeless. We have the ability to float from one climate controlled box to the next, our distress smoothed over by Ritalin and Prozac, until we forget that we are inescapably linked to the rest of the world. Nonetheless, Drengson wisely acknowledges that we have moved beyond the traditional egalitarian hunter–gatherer societies of the past and we cannot return to them fully. We must work within the current order if we want to initiate positive changes. These changes begin within our own minds before branching out into the physical world. Rather than leaving technology behind, we can design more sustainable, Earth-conscious technology. A shift in our thinking, motivated by a true connection to our intimate ecosystems, will help us make these decisions.

Drengson believes that a fifth wave of spiritual beliefs is taking shape in modern society. He describes future primitivism (see LaChapelle, 1978) and Neo-paganism (see DiZerga, 2001) as examples of this new spirituality. Primitive spiritual awareness arose in hunter–gatherer and rural societies through direct contact with the natural world. In modern days, those who do not have constant access to these wild places are developing a *neo-primal* awareness (see p. 123) birthed in the heart of a technologically dependent society.

In Chapter 6, "Ceremonial Dance Journeys", Drengson uses contemporary trance dancing (Raves) as an example of a neo-primal ceremonial art. He asks the question, "Can high-tech sound and chemical entheogens get us back to Nature and the sacred?" (p. 116) He describes the spiritual space that may be attained through rhythm, ecstasy, and communal dancing. Many of his examples are taken from his own participation at various trance dance events. The resulting eclectic fusion of electronic and natural music "leads us back to nature, even though it started in the city" (p. 116). He suggests certain modifications to the Rave structure that would make it more like a shamanic ceremony.

The *Wild Way Home* is a motivational text. It reminds the reader to spend more time actually walking in a forest and less time reading about walking in the forest. Drengson explains that book knowledge is useless by itself, because "authentic knowledge is grounded in firsthand experience" (p. 214). The teachings in this book are useless without applied discipline, regular practice, and experiential knowledge. For example, no amount of advanced scientific explanation can replace the actual experience of interacting with a wild creature. A special television series cannot express all of the implicit qualities of a mule deer. No book, regardless of the writer's talent, can ever communicate the true experience of looking a deer directly in the eyes.

Drengson's writing itself is a skillful example of a Whole Art. He utilizes an accordant amalgamation of personal, academic, literary, and religious sources to support and explain his methods. Drengson is inspired by Naess's deep ecology movement (see Naess, 2002; Drengson 1995) as well as Muir's poetic prose, by Jesus's "Sermon on the Mount" and the song of a Swainson's thrush. This book would feel at home sandwiched between Carson's *Silent Spring* (Carson, 1962) and Thich Nhat Hanh's *The Miracle of Mindfulness* (1991). *Wild Way Home* is appropriate for a wide audience—from a class on ecopsychology to a local reading group. I would love to see this book in the hands of a major industrial CEO.

—Tanya Collings

References

Carson, R. (1962). *Silent spring.* New York, New York: Houghton Mifflin.

DiZerega, G. (2001). *Pagans and Christians: The spiritual experience.* St. Paul MN: Llewellyn Publishers.

Drengson, A. (2010). *Wild way home: Spiritual life in the 3rd millennium.* Victoria, BC, Canada: Lightstar Press.

Drengson, A. & Inoue, Y. (Eds.) (1995). *The deep ecology movement: An introductory anthology.* Berkley, CA: North Atlantic Books.

Hanh, T. N. (1991). *The Miracle of mindfulness.* Boston, MA: Beacon Press.

LaChapelle, D. (1978). *Earth wisdom.* Silverton, CO: Finn Hill Arts.

TANYA COLLINGS is a freelance editor and writer. She is currently employed as the Assistant Editor of *Anthropology of Consciousness* and Assistant Editor of *Restoration Earth*. In order to connect more closely to the natural world, Tanya has been living in a canvas tent in Boulder Town, Utah, for the past three years. Contact: aocjournal@usu.edu

Unbroken

Anne Westlund

Westlund, A. (2011). Unbroken. *Restoration Earth: An Interdisciplinary Journal for the Study of Nature & Civilization*, 1(1), 99. Copyright © The Authors. All rights reserved. For reprint information contact: oceanseminary@verizon.net.

My world
a flat white plane
as far as the eye can see.

Traversing this lonely place
like a mountain climber or aerialist
holding on with just my feet,
against the pull of gravity.

This meaningless trek
that I must take from here to there
all my activities
just as nonsensical.

I must have a place here
in His image.
Why must it be this place?

When will I enter a new landscape?

(like an ant on a white-painted wall)

When will other vistas be within reach?

I cry quietly, or pray out loud,
alone on this plain, unbroken.
I too, am unbroken.

Unbroken.

Letting Go

Lynne Elson

Elson, L. (2011). Letting go. *Restoration Earth: An Interdisciplinary Journal for the Study of Nature & Civilization, 1*(1), 100–101. Copyright © The Authors. All rights reserved. For reprint information contact: oceanseminary@verizon.net.

"Lord knows I don't know what I'm doing. I hope somebody comes and helps me off this reef." Carole's kayak was stuck in the mud. Sea kelp grabbed at her paddle, pulling it under. "Why is this happening to me?"

Carole wanted to scream, to call out to her tour group but they were gliding further and further away without her. She forgot the guide's name and didn't feel comfortable calling out in distress. She wanted to get out of this by herself. That is why she was out here, to get back in touch with her strength.

Kaz took five years of her life and left her without warning. She came home one day to an apartment that looked like her apartment minus a few pounds. She couldn't put her finger on what was missing until her neighbor, Monique knocked on her door. In a whisper, Monique asked if everything was all right. "I saw Kaz take the dresser and a few boxes. I had no idea you guys were breaking up." Carole's heart jumped into her throat. She ran into the bedroom and headed straight for the closet. His side was empty. But he left his computer. Carole sat down and logged on. It took forever to turn on, but when it did, she saw it. *The note.* Monique sat down and read over Carole's shoulder. It said that he wasn't happy and needed a change. Carole stood up, unplugged the monitor and heaved it out the window. Monique put a hand on Carole's shoulder. "He wasn't good enough for you. I always knew that."

It was Monique's idea for Carole to go on a tour of Catalina Island. Monique had honeymooned there a few years ago and raved about its serene beaches and gorgeous coral reefs.

The tour group was out of sight now and Carole began to panic. Tears formed in her eyes when her paddle sank out of reach. Now what would she do? Would the tour come back for her? Would she have to swim back to shore? She was a good swimmer, but how many miles was it back to shore? Aren't there sharks in the Pacific Ocean? She allowed herself a long moment to cry.

Carole had not cried about Kaz's leaving. She was too angry for that. She did play it over and over in her mind. As she left for work, he said, "Love ya" and hugged her goodbye. Does that sound like a man who had a moving van coming that afternoon?

Carole screamed into the endless open air. "Why?" Carole waited for some kind of answer. There was none. Not a stir. Not even a breeze in response. Carole was irrefutably alone.

Her mind was unsteady. What made her think she could do this? Her only paddling experience was a few times on the very calm Delaware and Raritan canal near home. Never was there any fear of being stranded or stuck. There were always joggers passing by on the trail above her. Here, so far from everything and everyone she knows, Carole had to rely on her own inner guidance. She decided to jump into the water and take charge of the tangle of vines around her paddle. Unfortunately the vines had another idea. They did not want to let go so easily. Tired of feeling defeated, she dove down toward the paddle and pulled, ripped and tugged as much as she could. It wasn't long until Carole knew this was a bad idea.

Her hair tangled with the reef and seaweed. Her eyes burned and she couldn't get up to breathe. Not too far away was a stick. Carole grabbed onto it and fought for her life. She slammed the stick over and over to clear away the muck that engulfed her. The more she pushed, the more it pushed back. She needed more strength, so she called upon all the women who came before her, who understood her feeling of abandonment, the ones left at the altar or left to care for their children alone. Even with the strength of a hundred women, Carole's battle ended in a knot of flesh and sea. Carole couldn't fight anymore. She knew this was it; this was how she was going to die. She gave into it.

She thought of Kaz, his smile, the way his chestnut hair fell softly over one eye, the time he brought her soup when she was sick, and she let go of the anger. She loved him once, but no longer. She let go of the sinking feeling that she dragged around which made her think she could have done something: loved more, paid more attention. Let him keep the toilet seat up. Then she let go of all her sadness. Let go of her fear of being alone. Let go of her need to be the best. Let go of her anger toward her sister who flaunted her success in Carole's face as if it they were still teenagers and going out for the Cheerleading squad. It was as if she was letting go of clothing—she felt lighter, smoother, less smothered than she had in years.

Before saying goodbye to the world, Carole looked at the stick she held in her hand and realized that it was hollow. She could breathe through the stick. She tried it and a little bit of air and some water came in. Then she tried again and she could breathe. She was stuck under the water but she could breathe.

Carole's eyes weren't burning anymore. She watched as the fish swam around her curiously. They came out of their protective dens behind the coral walls. They swam with one eye on her, checking to see if she was friend or foe. They were gorgeous, full of the brightest colors and most amazing patterns. A bright blue and gold fish swam right up to her eye and looked deep within her. Any tension that was still within her body released as she breathed, floated, and stared at the fish. It was as if she understood what it was like to be a fish, just going with the ebb and flow of life. She felt the ocean rocking her into a calm she hadn't felt since she was in the womb. She wanted to stay there staring at this fish forever.

Soon she felt the tide change and her hair untangled. She noticed that if she waited until the water was just right she could free herself a little bit more. She waited. When the tides turned and calmed, she untangled her arms from the seaweed's grasp. Then her legs. The paddle bobbed up toward her, just out of reach. When the water was just right, she could grab that too.

Carole smiled and felt a little silly as she thanked the fish and then the ocean for their help. She swam toward the top of the ocean. When her head cleared the water, she gasped, finding it hard to breathe normally. It took her a few moments to remember how. She tugged the boat and paddle away from the web of kelp to a clear spot of ocean. She kicked as hard as she could and found herself able to climb up on her kayak again. Soon she was sitting upright and grabbed her oar. Winded and only one scrape on her ankle from the reef, Carole had come out of this test pretty much unscathed. In fact she felt stronger than she ever did in her life.

"I did it," Carole thought over and over again. "Thank you." She wasn't sure who she was thanking, but she was thankful all the same. With each stroke to freedom a laugh bubbled up from deep within her, a youthful giggle that she hadn't let loose since she played tag and did log-rolls on the playground hills. Carole knew she was healed, but even more than that she was happy.

Note: An earlier version of this story was published in the ezine *World Riot* in 2008.

LYNNE ELSON is an award winning playwright and much sought after teacher. Her plays have been produced across the United States. Lynne is proud to be the Artistic Director of the NOW Theatre Company based in Central New Jersey. She is also a member of the Passage Theatre Playwrights Unit, an involvement that helped inspire her to write *Crazy, Crazy on You,* which had a successful run in the 2011 Philly Fringe Festival. Her one-act play *Stolen Glorie* was the winner of the Great Platte River Playwrights Festival (2001) and will be performed as a full-length in NOW Theatre Company's inaugural season. Check out her two monologue books for teens entitled *Girls Rule!* and *Guys Rule!* published by Meriwether Publishing. Another crowd pleaser is her multicultural festive play, *Holiday Shmoliday* which you can find online at Playscripts.com. When not writing, Lynne is walking her furry baby, Harrison, with husband, singer/songwriter, Anker or creating videos for her blog: *The Adventures of Yoga Girl and Swami Cat*. Visit her online at LynneElson.com.

My Town

Anne Westlund

Westlund, A. (2011). My town. *Restoration Earth: An Interdisciplinary Journal for the Study of Nature & Civilization*, *1*(1), 102. Copyright © The Authors. All rights reserved. For reprint information contact: oceanseminary@verizon.net.

Above the hum of machinery
the sound of cars rushing by
I can hear the birds
as if in defiance.

There are still bugs
despite all the disinfectants,
weed-killer, napalm.

Dogs roam free
in our neighborhood.
They come up to say hello
or bark their freedom
at their fellows behind fences.

There are more slugs every year
it seems like.
The rain brings them
in the morning, in the grass
almost a convention.

And the deer
not hunted here
in this unnatural setting
eat weeds next to the post office
four of them, a family portrait.
Frustrated hunters
with gun racks in their trucks
have to stop
as they cross the road.

*biography on page 34

"Resting" copyright © 2011 by Anne Westlund. Photo taken in Washington State, USA.

Restoration Earth Issue 2, Spring 2012

Ecofeminism

RE is now accepting academic and artistic submissions exploring the diverse perspectives embedded within ecofeminism. Submission deadline is March 1, 2012. Additionally if you are interested in reviewing books, movies, or music that are linked to the theme, please let us know. A reminder: academic papers should be written in APA (we will accept other formats). Our website may host videos and music; while our print journal accepts all printable artwork and written material. Please contact Dr. Batten (MacDowell) for further details at oceanseminary@verizon.net